NEITHER ESCAPING NOR EXPLOITING SEX

Janette Gray RSM

NEITHER ESCAPING NOR EXPLOITING SEX
Women's celibacy

NEITHER ESCAPING NOR EXPLOITING SEX:
Women's celibacy
© Janette Gray RSM, 1995
First published in Australia, August 1995, by
ST PAULS, 60-70 Broughton Road, Homebush, NSW 2140

All rights reserved

No part of this book may be reproduced or transmitted in any form or by any means, electronic or mechanical, including photocopying, recording, or by any information storage and retrieval system without permission in writing from the Publisher

Cover design: Bruno Colombari SSP

Published in the United Kingdom
by arrangement with ST PAULS/AUSTRALIA

This edition for sale in Europe only

ST PAULS
Middlegreen, Slough SL3 6BT, United Kingdom
Moyglare Road, Maynooth, Co. Kildare, Ireland

ISBN 085439 519 9

Printed by The Guernsey Press Co. Ltd, Guernsey, C.I.

ST PAULS is an activity of the priests and brothers of the Society of St Paul who proclaim the Gospel through the media of social communication

In memory of my mother
Patricia Mary Gray
1928-1992

'Did not our hearts burn within us...' Luke 24:32

Acknowledgments

Extracts reprinted from:
New Wineskins: Re-imagining religious life today, by Sandra Schneiders IHM. Used by permission of Paulist Press, Mahwah, NJ, USA.
'Celibacy or Consummation in the Garden', by Gary Anderson, in *Harvard Theological Review* 82, © 1989 by the President and Fellows of Harvard College, Cambridge, Mass, USA. Reprinted by permission.
God and the Rhetoric of Sexuality, by Phyllis Trible, copyright © 1978 Fortress Press. Used by permission of Augsburg Fortress, Minneapolis, USA.
The Prophetic Imagination by Walter Brueggemann, copyright © 1978, Fortress Press. Used by permission of Augsburg Fortress, Minneapolis, USA.
Embodiment by James B. Nelson, copyright © 1978, Augsburg Publishing House. Used by permission of Augsburg Fortress, Minneapolis, USA.
In This Motherless Geography, by Elaine Orr, © 1987, first published in Fall edition of *Journal of Feminist Studies in Religion*, Cambridge, Mass, USA. Used by permission of the author.
Sexism and God-Talk, by Rosemary Radford Ruether © 1983, 1993, Beacon Press, Boston, USA. Used by permission.
A Passion for Friends, by Janice Raymund © 1986, Beacon Press, Boston, USA, and The Women's Press, London, UK. Used by permission.
To Change the World, by Rosemary Radford Ruether, 1983, SCM Press, London, UK. Used by permission.
In Memory of Her, by Elisabeth Schüssler-Fiorenza, 1983, SCM Press, London, UK. Used by permission.
The Relative Contributions of Personality, Social Network, and Cognitive Processes to the Experience of Loneliness in Mature Aged Women, by Margaret Smith, unpublished thesis, Swinburne Institute of Technology, Melbourne, 1988. Used by permission.
Poems, by Anne Waugh, in *Listen: Journal of the Institute of the Sisters of Mercy of Australia*, vol 8, 1989, 23. Used by permission.
Every effort has been made to procure copyright on all sources used in this book. Apologies are made for any infringement.

Contents

	Acknowledgments	9
	Introduction	11
1.	Celibacy's denial of sexuality	15
	Women's experience of celibacy	17
2.	A new reading of the traditional metaphors of celibacy	29
	The Song of Songs	32
	The Gospel of John	42
	The prophet Jeremiah	52
	New metaphors for women's celibacy	61
3.	Sexuality and women's celibacy	63
	Embodied celibacy	64
	Political celibacy	69
	Inclusive celibacy	72
4.	Socio-theology of women's celibacy	77
	Women reclaiming the incarnation	82
	Women reclaiming the struggle	97
	Women reclaiming symbols	108
	Women reclaiming the community of life	117

8 • Neither escaping nor exploiting sex

5. Ecology of celibacy   125
   Death: the ecological problem   128
   The un-ecological aspect of christianity   134
   Celibacy has a prophetic purpose   143
   Embodiment and interconnectedness   151
   After the distancing   156

   Conclusion   159

   Bibliography   165

   Index   173

Acknowledgments

This project has shown me how credible and valuable religious vowed celibacy is. I hope it is as convincing for you. It is the lives and reflections of the many women I interviewed that have made this possible. I am deeply grateful to all the sisters who generously shared very personal experiences and insights. They said much more than this work can convey. What began as a personal need to understand celibacy more became a fascinating conversation with many warm and searching women of faith. This study was practically and very personally supported by my congregation leader Sr Patricia Pak Poy. My friends and companions in Mercy community Sisters Joan Haren, Rosemary Day, Ruth Egar, Monica Marks, Deirdre O'Connor, Carmel Bourke, Anne Gregory, Gemma Johnson, Mary Anne Duigan, Margaret Abbott, Christine Keain and the Angas Street Sisters listened for hours and never visibly gave up hope. I thank my other community in West Perth led by Sr Beverley Stott who gave me space and encouragement in dark hours, especially Sisters Mary O'Connor, Norma Scheikowsky, Kaye Bolwell and Joan Flynn. Sr Sharon Price and the North Sydney Mercies, the Mercy sisters of Melbourne and Ballarat East, Perth, Brisbane, Rockhampton, Cairns, Townsville and Grafton invited me to share this work at different stages of its development. Their responses and the interview approach suggested by Sr Rosemary Crumlin (Parramatta Mercies) substantially enhanced the outcome.

The late Rev Dr John Gaden sensitively guided my thesis in what were unexpectedly to be the last months of his life. His death was a significant personal loss for me, but a much greater tragedy for Christianity in Australia. John and Janet Gaden were modelling a mutual 'community of life' well before I read about it. Dr Michael Jackson bravely took up supervision of my masters thesis, believed in what I was trying to do and taught me how to make better sense of it. Fr Adrian Lyons SJ helped me edit it from a thesis to something more interesting to read. Many thanks to Rosemary Day RSM for overseeing its publication.

Most of all, I wish to thank my parents Roger and Patricia. Their love and mutuality have always embodied for me the faithfulness of God. Mum asked the question that began this search for better understanding of women's celibacy. I'm sure she knew better than I where it would all lead.

Introduction

'Neither escaping nor exploiting sex,
they embrace and enjoy it.
Their love is truly bone of bone and flesh of flesh,
and this image of God male and female
is indeed very good.'
Phyllis Trible on the *Song of Songs*[1]

Despite the Biblical approval of human sexuality in the *Song of Songs*, vowed religious celibacy renounces sexual union. Over the centuries religious celibates have read the *Song of Songs* as an analogy of their virginal 'spiritual marriage' to God. Yet the *Song of Songs* celebrates a very sexual image of eschatological hope. Reflecting the holiness of creation, the human companionship of sexual union and procreation completes the divine design. This is in contrast with a theology of renunciation that spurns sex and escapes it for a purity that is meant more to resemble God — the creator of sex!

---

1 Phyllis Trible, *God and the Rhetoric of Sexuality*, Philadelphia: Fortress, 1978, 161.

Religious chastity or celibacy has always been defined in opposition. Celibacy is seen as against what is physical, against the world, against the sensual, against sex and marriage. Being spiritual and other-worldly, it is pure and intact – like God. But *is* God like that? Denied of any positive exploration and assessment, this anti-view of celibacy has ruled. In a world that does not share such a negative view of sex, how can celibacy make any sense? As Jacques Pohier judges:

> Depriving oneself of what is represented by human love and sexuality at the end of the twentieth century cannot have the same significance as depriving oneself of what they represented in the thirteenth century, and such a course of action runs a serious risk of making quite different statements about God and the human condition from what one would want to signify or believe that one was signifying, in such renunciation.[2]

Too often religious celibacy gets smothered under the Church's strong focus on the obligatory clerical discipline of celibacy. Despite this, clerical celibacy is not identical with the celibacy of vowed religious life: it is a Church discipline incorporated into the priestly life, while celibacy with poverty and obedience is integral to the vowed forms of religious life. So the exclusively male clerical understanding of celibacy has become universally applied. The experience of female and male religious celibates has been hidden behind the problems of clerical celibacy. One result is the difference between women's and men's celibacy is denied. Because women's sexuality and femininity have been traditionally implicated with sin and in the 'Fall of

---

2   Jacques Pohier, *God – In Fragments*, London: SCM, 1985, 33.

man', female celibacy means more than a female version of male physical or social renunciation of sex. Virginity in a woman requires 'a far more profound demand for alienation and renunciation of self than any demand for continence on the part of men'.[3]

Women's understanding and lived experience of post-Vatican II religious life is also different to male and male clerical religious life. As Sandra Schneiders observes 'women's religious congregations have already gone farther than any other group *as a group* in the Church toward grasping the radicality of the contemporary crises in the areas of spiritual renewal and social justice'.[4] While women religious were so preoccupied with service of God, God's people and Church they could not develop a theologically expressed understanding of celibacy from their specific gender viewpoint. How have so many women lived celibacy when its theology is so negative and impoverished of their gender experience? Can women's sexual understanding contribute something to the theology of celibacy? Is it possible to live positively such a negatively defined life? Is there any connection between the God of life and the God people follow by living celibacy?

Celibacy has been bound too long to a dualism that distorts and silences the lived reality of religious celibates. By identifying and valuing the particular celibate experience of women, I believe that the incarnational and eschatological meaning of celibacy can be better communicated for our times. This way claims can be made for celibacy

---

[3] Elizabeth Castelli, Virginity and its Meaning for Women's Sexuality in Early Christianity, *Journal of Feminist Studies in Religion* 2, 1986, 85-6.
[4] Sandra Schneiders, *New Wineskins: Re-imagining Religious life Today*, New York: Paulist, 1986, 14.

that are not exclusive or against other lifestyles, but which recognise those distinctive qualities of celibacy that enrich the diversity of all life. So, like the redeemed Paradise couple of the *Song of Songs*, women's experience of celibacy can be known for its embracing and joyful commitment to 'neither escaping nor exploiting sex'.

1

Celibacy's denial of sexuality

*'If we mean anything by "incarnation" the notion involves caring for bodies —
feeding, healing and delighting in them.'*
Rosemary Haughton[1]

Until now, Religious vowed celibacy has lacked an adequate positive theology. Those theologies available to religious men and women in the Catholic Church fail to deal with human experience and sexuality. They also fail to answer the challenges posed by the Second Vatican Council, which emphasised 'the universal call to holiness' rather than 'the life of perfection' as lived through the vows of Poverty, Chastity (or Celibacy) and Obedience;[2] The Council came to understand the Church as committed to the world, dedicated to reading within ordinary experience 'the signs of the times'.[3] A theology of world renunciation, that

---

1   Rosemary Haughton, *The Re-Creation of Eve*, Springfield: Templegate, 1985, 41.
2   *Lumen Gentium* (Vatican II Constitution on the Church), chapter 5, nos 39-41. *Vatican Council II: The Conciliar and Post Conciliar Documents*, Austin Flannery ed., Dublin: Dominican Publications, 1975.
3   *Gaudium et Spes*, no 4.

Church people were meant to live in isolation, outside history and society, was left aside.

The terms chastity, celibacy and virginity often appear as interchangeable, even though their meaning is different. Their use can be ambiguous. Christianity has employed chastity to refer to sexual abstinence except in marriage and continence within marriage. When also applied to the vowed religious evangelical counsel, confusion results. All Christians are required to be chaste, but chastity is the vow some Christians make. Virginity while a common condition for those in religious life is not necessary nor a pre-condition for the vow of chastity. Celibacy is also ambiguously applied to the religious life vow, to temporary commitment to sexual abstinence outside of religious life and to the clerical discipline attached to Catholic priesthood. Despite this celibacy does unambiguously mean no sex and is the more readily understood term for vowed religious sexual abstinence. This confusion is a reflection of the problem of universally applied and inappropriate terms and the changing understanding of human sexuality in the Church.

For religious women especially, a gulf exists between their experience of celibacy as a Christian vocation and its theological definition. My own suspicion and disquiet intensified when I realised how ill-fitted these theologies actually are to this experience. From the accounts that religious women give of their lives, celibacy emerges as something rich, positive and confidently human though one would not guess this from writings on celibacy.

If celibacy is perceived simply as sexual deprivation, what follows is distorted human development, social unease and perhaps even a kind of irresponsibility. If celibacy is viewed as an escapist lifestyle, and one most at home in an institution, it will be dismissed as anachronistic and romantic religiosity. It is distressing enough to find celibacy misunderstood and mocked by those with world views that discount any sexual abstinence. But such negative views also persist within the Church and religious congregations, particularly with regard to women's celibacy. In my view, the problem with celibacy is not that it is irrelevant nor out of date. The problem is that those who live it lack the means to communicate its meaning adequately. Often celibates retreat into mystery or the privacy of their own experience and thereby censor this experience. Negativity feeds on such defensiveness. Some of the sisters I interviewed for this study feared that of course I would conclude that celibacy is impossible, invalid, or irrelevant. This was despite these same celibate women insisting on the value of their own lives! Fearing that celibacy cannot withstand examination even from friendly sources, its true believers retreat into mystification.

Women's experience of celibacy

Most people find celibacy a stumbling-block. They are also unable to understand the point of the religious life. Whenever religious sisters try to explain their lives, the response is usually incredulous and dismissive. Even more experienced celibates often cannot adequately communicate the meaning of their lifestyle. An early draft of a statement on celibacy from my religious congregation, the Sisters of Mercy, was as static, elusive and unconvincing as any of the literature I had read on celibacy.[4] Worse, I found it

---

4   This became the ISMA 1988 National Chapter Statement: 'Celibacy: "A Lifetime Burning in Each Moment".' The final document was much more

fundamentally contradicted my experience. It was timeless, outside of any culture, and asexual — in other words, safely cocooned in otherworldly disembodied mystification. Around that time on a long journey, my mother questioned me about why I am a celibate. She knew all the traditional Catholic theology of celibacy, but could not associate it with me. I found I could not communicate anything to replace it. It became imperative to find a way of understanding and describing my experience of celibacy.

My quest became focused around a number of suspicions to do with the negative presentation of celibacy. While many people recognise that marriage is not a blissful existence, very few deny that it has any meaning, or assume that it automatically distorts all human development. In contrast, celibacy is universally suspected to be too negative to allow normal human development, to be a haven for sexual aversion or sexual deviance, and to be useless as a lifestyle (except as a way for the sexually experienced to avoid contracting AIDS). I was particularly intrigued that celibacy is deemed to be so unnatural. To be sure, the dualist anti-sexual framework of traditional Catholic morality provides some justification for a rejection of sexual activity and procreative function in celibacy. But, this is not convincing either in a sex-focused world or in a Church more incarnational in its theology. Also, I became more conscious of the inability of celibates to explain the value of their lifestyle and their tendency to recoil into its 'mystery' or their privacy. This does not fit with the public nature of vowed religious life. I also became suspicious

developed and aware of these issues. *ISMA Second National Chapter Acts and Proceedings*, Sydney: ISMA, 1988, 7.

about why celibate women particularly have to apologise and for their existence, as if somehow they have deeply betrayed their biological and social purpose as women?

All these negative responses to the phenomenon of celibacy contradict the theological harmony claimed for celibacy in the literature about religious life. On the basis of my own experience I also knew that many celibate women are warm, loving and sexually conscious, living in integrity and harmony with other humans and God. There was more to be known about women's experience of celibacy. As my individual experience seemed too small to represent these lives, I decided to interview a sample of sisters from different congregations of my own order to provide an homogeneous but broader range of experience. As my task was more theological than sociological or quantitative, I decided against a more random varied sample. My interest was not in surveying diversity, i.e. being neither representative nor comprehensive, but in hearing and interpreting (through our common language) how these sisters made meaning out of their celibate lives.[5] I interviewed and held group discussions with over eighty Sisters of Mercy from seventeen congregations in Australia. Those interviewed were surprisingly generous with both their understanding and experience. Rather than repeating the dualistic renunciations of published theologies of celibacy,

---

5   My selection criteria for the sample were extremely idiosyncratic. I chose articulate and reflective women from a wide age range – 26-84 years old – with examples from each half-decade.Those I chose appeared at some ease with themselves as women and with their celibate life. Despite such a small and personal sample, I am convinced that the wide variety of experience and responses from them reveals such diversity that it is hard to imagine what more could exist across a wider range of religious celibate women.

they spoke realistically and vividly of their lives as celibate women. I found their observations affirmed that celibate experience is natural and, while different, more like than unlike other women's experience.

Most of the celibate women I interviewed revealed that their sole opportunities for developing a personal appreciation of celibacy came through the deep challenges of experiencing intimacy and loneliness. In contrast, reading or attending seminars on celibacy provided only underdeveloped and irrelevant theory. This had frightened them off sharing their experience. Many sisters regularly confronted with having to explain their celibacy also recalled the difficulty in finding an appropriate level of disclosure. How do you share what is most real to you, personally, spiritually and sexually, without it appearing either a curiosity, seductive or a problem. Most of the sisters interviewed felt they lacked confidence and opportunities for sharing their celibate experience. Yet one sister saw this as positively contributing to developing her understanding of celibacy:

> 'The great experience is that you have had to learn celibacy yourself because the retreats, books and sharing told you so little about it. You found out about it yourself by experience. That's why it's so rich now because we learnt it ourselves and didn't just absorb others' explanations.' (51 years)[6]

Very few had experienced free discussion of their celibacy or sexuality within community structures or with others outside of religious life.

---

[6] The following quotes from the interviews identify the age of the respondent in parathenses.

Celibacy's denial of sexuality • 21

> 'Thinking about sex was a "bad thought", therefore a sin. That was bad enough, but to talk about it to others, you wouldn't even think of it.' (62)

> 'It's impossible to find someone you can trust to talk to in a sense that you feel comfortable, not judged.' (49)

> 'You can't really be too honest, because they might be frightened.' (51)

> 'I felt alone and it was extremely painful. Support came from another female member of staff. She taught me about not taking the law too seriously — she was a free kind of person and I was not.' (59)

All expressed how celibacy had been important in their lives, even though most had not set out to be celibate, but only as part of the religious life they chose.

> 'Celibacy for me was part of a package. I wanted to be a nun to work for the message of the kingdom and this was the only way I knew at the time, so you took the whole thing.' (54)

> 'If you could be in this set-up and be married I'd probably go for it. I haven't got a sense of choosing to be celibate, I chose a life with these women, and the vows went along with it.' (39)

A few said that they did not think about celibacy too much, while the majority had found it very costly and particularly difficult at different stages in their lives. Women in their late twenties, late thirties, forties and early fifties particularly expressed the personal and social cost of the demands of celibacy.

> 'I've found it hard and I've found a freedom in it. I've had to battle with it all my life.' (54)

'When you get older things hit you more. Different times when you feel things more — life is a number of cycles — of tired, of lonely cycles." (65)

'The older you get, the harder celibacy gets.' (50)

'I chose to enter into a deeply sexual relationship, which took its course. I felt some guilt about that. I viewed it as an act of defiance against the structures of the celibate institution I was not happy in. I was struggling not so much with celibacy as with the concept and reality of the religious life I was very angry with.' (29)

'There's a kind of static self-denial that can be associated with celibacy. It's very hard most of the time, so I wouldn't want to glorify anything of it.' (44)

'It must be carried very consciously as an ongoing choice that is a painful loneliness that is a decision for an ideal.' (39)

Most reported that interpersonal relationships, particularly with males (these were often also celibates), helped their self-understanding and appreciation of their celibacy.

'I know I'm lovable. I've had experiences of it and it's formed me to trust myself personally with others, not just with one person. These have been good experiences and I see celibacy as a loving experience.' (42)

'I don't have any ways to explain it except that it's about entering into relationships at all sorts of levels, that helps me to make meaning of living in a celibate way.' (44)

'I really felt God's presence in that intense relationship somehow. Up until then I'd always done the right thing so God would love me. This was an invitation to love God and to trust that it all was OK. I look back to that as a real turning point. And I think my relationship with other people changed, and I really had a lot more understanding of people and their problems.' (59)

'You never really get rid of all the sexual drives or the desires. Celibacy has only been possible through relationships and friendships, and that has mostly been beyond community.' (54)

This sample did not present as a sad group of deprived women. Some did express loneliness and a sense of incompleteness, even to the extent of regret. A few could not recommend the lifestyle, but most had found meaning in their loneliness and had somehow integrated deep and long term relationships.

'In intense moments times of fairly intense relationship with men mostly (but not exclusively) that's emotional, companionship or even physical — I wonder why am I choosing to be celibate? and what makes me think there's anything better in not being sexually involved than in being sexually involved?' (56)

'For a long time I didn't have an experience or relationship like that — the whole relationship has helped me because I'd be a lot less a woman and a lot less a celibate if I didn't know him.' (58)

'If you didn't have friends in the group, who would you come "home" to? There should be a "home" where you can come home, where you feel good, your friends are going to be there.' (65)

'I learnt in this relationship that there is so much more to me that I may never have known had I not loved celibately.' (33)

The sample did not reveal any one type of celibate woman. Many would still desire bearing and nurturing their own children, while some had little interest in birthing and parenting.

'There have been times when I've really deeply wanted to have a child and really wanted to experience childbirth, and wanted that fullness of my body potential to be.' (44)

'I regret that I have not known a relationship like that. I regret that I haven't loved someone so completely. I wonder what that's done to me — that I haven't allowed that to come to its fruition, sort of pursued it as being something good.' (48)

A few expressed what they called a 'selfish' desire for space and solitude in their lives that would preclude marriage or family.

'I wouldn't have been a good mother, I mean, I'm too selfish, I want my own time too much. Peace and quiet are too important for me.' (39)

The majority expressed a keen desire for the support and comfort of a sustained partnership, particularly when they were lonely or stressed by their ministries.

'The experience of incompleteness: that there isn't someone with whom I share my life very closely day by day in that very total way. Especially when my work is very difficult or even very on the edge. You come out of it and then it hits you, the place of one person for *you*.' (55)

None were recluses, but a few insisted on their utter need for solitude.[7] Many, in contrast, emphasised the advantage of a few or many close relationships with men and other women. Few admitted feeling defined by males and the necessity for them of a relationship with a male. Many described how their human development had been particularly enhanced by relationships with women.

'I realise that my friendship with other women is really important, through them I've come to an unexpected sense

---

[7] This may be an effect of the criteria of the sample.

of myself as woman experiencing myself as part of a vital group.' (41)

'A long relationship with a male had a lot to do with my self-development. When it ended I felt bereft of the male in my life ... I don't think I got my true sense of my self being woman from that relationship as much as from other women.' (55)

'I found a lot of women in our community, cultured and very progressive – they opened up life for me. Particularly the older women kind of nurtured me.' (62)

None admitted not liking men. Experience with men was varied, both in degree, length and time in life. Sisters over 45 years generally had less experience with male relationships before they entered religious life but often had significant relationships with males during their early years as sisters. Despite the restrictions of pre-Vatican II convent life, a large number interviewed knew and were in frequent contact with men, through schools, parishes and the community life of a locality.

'In my twenties I suffered a prevailing feeling of loneliness, because of the system. I had heterosexual relationships before I joined, so I was open to that. We only saw priests, and they couldn't relate very well. The loneliness was probably partly separation from men.' (55)

"When I was young I would have fallen for men a few times. I would feel devastated when they moved away.' (66)

"The sense of falling in love with him but feeling that it all fitted with my life and with his life, because he was celibate and a priest and I enjoyed his view of the Church and I could share my views. My sense of that was it supported me in my life – it was a good relationship because we could help one another in the Church.' (48)

Sexual experience was varied. Many admitted to physical expression in their most meaningful relationships, and a few had engaged in some 'genital exploration'. Some had been in sexually active relationships, but many of these had been short-lived. Many of these women spoke consciously in body and sexual terminology about themselves.

> 'It takes a hell of a lot of honesty, sensitivity and awareness of what's really going on in your body, what's really going on in your heart.' (39)

> 'I can't live without some real affection — I'm not sure that God created us like that — with hormones, drives and sexual attraction.' (49)

> 'The question for me is integration: how can I pull together this big drive I have to be a full, loving, human woman and yet leave out such an obvious route into that as sexuality ?' (56)

> 'I feel a very sexual sort of being and I feel proud about that.' (55)

Very few described their experience piously. Many spoke of their inability to find solace or satisfaction for their needs exclusively through their relationship with God.

> 'Some women get extremely spiritual as a response to their celibacy — spiritualised out of existence. Then everything gets spiritualised out of the experience of one's life — they spiritualise all their female emotions and come out of it fairly badly.' (59)

> 'I don't know that it should take you out of the world it shouldn't because it's for the world.' (65)

> 'I think that other people have had to lead me to that place where I would seek recourse in God, because sometimes God's the last one I would want to take recourse in, especially if I'm feeling vulnerable in a crisis or a hard place in living out my celibacy.' (44)

With few exceptions, most declared that their appreciation of the value of their celibacy came as much through other human relationships as through prayer and solitude. All insisted, though, on the necessity of a deep personal relationship with God to sustain celibate life.

> 'Because you're a celibate you experience more frequently the aloneness everyone knows. From that stems your greatest prayer because it's in that loneliness you seek out a more spiritual life. Otherwise I don't think you can cope with it. I think it would eat you away and turn you bitter.' (46)

> 'It is essential to have a capacity for mysticism. It's hard enough if that's there in you, but if you don't have that ability to draw from within to make sense out of it all, in the pain and the struggle, I don't know how people could live this way.' (39)

These celibate women do not conform to any one stereotype of social experience, family background, sexual preference, personality or body type. This diversity comes from both their individuality on entering religious life, and the inability of the repressive structures and spiritualities of pre-Vatican II religious life to manufacture a single type of celibate woman.

This broad summary indicates that popular and ecclesial stereotypes of the celibate do not fit these women. While the celibacy of religious life is judged as uniform and negative, the experience is as varied as any other human lifestyle. A combination of dualistic world-views, both in religious and secular cultures, and the continued inability of celibates to value and share publicly the meaning of their lives, sustains these accusations of deprivation, irresponsibility and anachronism. A negative and dualistic definition of celibacy is understandable from the world-view of a sex-obsessed culture. But celibates do not comply with this view.

The categorising of celibacy as unnatural has forced most celibates into a permanent posture of apology. Rather a critique of this dichotomy and its invalidity and its inapplicability is needed. One sister interviewed observed:

> 'If life has ways of looking after its own growth, and its own future, then celibacy is as natural as marriage, as having babies. The Church has never helped us to see it as natural — they've taught us to see it as *not* natural — not the natural way to go. Perhaps celibacy could be *the* natural lifestyle — we are all born celibate and many die celibate. That the majority seek to add marriage to their experience does not make the choice of the minority not natural.' (48)

From the viewpoint of their experience, celibates can rightly reject the pervasive negative perception of their lifestyle. Such confidence is grounded in recognising the value of their experience, as of *all* human experience. This does not discount the need for a critical assessment of whether celibacy is irresponsible towards humanity. Rather, it requires that celibate experience be critical about its contribution to human life and all life. Catholic theology and teaching has a history of suspicion of the value of human experience. It has taken a one-way approach to human relations 'as if its responsibility was to form and shape experience, but hardly ever be shaped by it.'[8] Acquaintance with the reality of women's experience of celibacy underlines its serious challenge to the negative established theology of celibacy.

---

8   R. McCormick, Moral Theology 1940-89: An Overview, *Theological Studies* 50, 1989, 20.

2

A new reading of the traditional metaphors of celibacy

> *'If History call me*
> *I may return, but not*
> *As I was.'*
>
> Elaine Orr[1]

Throughout the centuries religious life has been sustained by metaphors derived from biblical sources. Since the Second Vatican Council a number of Catholic scholars have examined the scriptures to provide a biblical basis for the vowed life, but these seem to have had limited influence on any theological restatement of the vowed religious life, particularly of celibacy. This was particularly evident in the preliminary papers for the Synod on Religious Life. Certain traditional metaphors recur in reference to celibacy. Reflecting on the symbolic character of celibacy, Sandra Schneiders calls celibacy an 'icon of a mystery'.[2] Before Vatican II, the metaphor for celibacy derived from spiritual

---

1 Elaine Orr, In this Motherless Geography, *Journal of Feminist Studies in Religion* 3, 1987, 97.
2 Schneiders', *New Wineskins: Re-Imagining Religious Life Today*, New York: Paulist, 1986, 114-136.

union as an alternative to marriage – the 'Bride of Christ'. This icon was drawn from the love poetry of the *Song of Songs*. It developed into a passionate image of the celibate's desire for total union with God. Socially, it fitted the celibate's need for particular belonging beyond the communal regimentation and anonymity prescribed in religious life. It afforded a personal and spiritual identity in a lifestyle that often denied the uniqueness of the person. In writing of more recent times, the 'Bride of Christ' icon is recast as 'unmarriageable for the sake of the kingdom'.[3]

Another expression of this understanding of celibacy was the New Testament cultic metaphor of 'Temple of the Holy Spirit' (also occurring as 'being in Christ' and 'indwelling'). The celibate understood her life as how a temple or holy place is a focused space for the divine presence and for union with the divinity. This metaphor avoided the more sublimated aspects of a spousal mystical union. Following the Second Vatican Council's reforms, the metaphor of prophetic sign or eschatological witness emerged. This was particularly popular during the decades of social reform and activism in the seventies. It also has biblical basis, yet this eschatological prophetism was applied more to the vows of poverty and obedience than to celibacy.

The persistence of these metaphors throughout history recommends them. Their rich background and wide adoption are good reasons for not abandoning them but rather mining them further for more meaning. Re-reading them

---

[3] e.g. E. Schillebeeckx, *Celibacy*; P. Van Breemen, *Called By Name*; Sandra M. Schneiders, Non-Marriage for the Sake of the Kingdom, *Widening the Dialogue: Reflections on Evangelica Testificatio*, Ottawa/Washington DC: Canadian Religious Conference/Leadership Conference of Women Religious, 1974, 125-197.

their biblical sources through feminist critical approaches can yield even more insights for a theology of celibacy.

This study of the metaphorical basis of the theology of celibacy requires a re-reading of these texts for their surplus of meanings rather than for some idealistic claim on the original intention of the text. 'What has to be appropriated is the meaning of the text itself, conceived in a dynamic way as the direction of thought opened up by the text.'[4] The metaphorical development of these texts in the past has been in 'the direction of thought opened up by the text'. The task of this re-reading is to continue the opening up of that direction of thought. This is to create a new word-event from the ongoing dialogue with the reality begun by the metaphors when they originally emerged from these texts.

Feminist criticism of biblical sources has revealed how the Judaeo-Christian canons can be liberative as well as having patriarchal limitations. This type of criticism disclaims a 'scientific' objectivity in relation to the texts it exegetes. Rather, it takes a partisan position. It enhances the traditional understanding of revelation by re-reading and reclaiming their under-side, women's experience. It identifies the patriarchal censorship of composition, selection, editing, translation and interpretation of the texts. Such a re-reading attempts a deconstruction of our usual approach to celibacy and a reconstruction of its metaphors through these texts. From the texts a perspective is drawn that includes women's experience today as essential data for any interpretation. While women are the subject of both

---

4 Paul Ricoeur, *Interpretation Theory: Discourse and the Surplus of Meaning*, Fort Worth: Texas Christian University Press, 1976, 92.

the *Song of Songs* and can be detected in the 'indwelling' material in John's Gospel, these texts are seldom interpreted in a way that values women's experience and sexuality. While women as well as men have identified with the more recent prophetic metaphor of celibacy this metaphor has not been derived from the example of the only celibate prophet, Jeremiah. Yet here may be an appropriate source for the prophetic metaphor of women's celibacy.

The *Song of Songs*

The Bride of Christ is one of the oldest Christian images associated with virginity and celibacy. Originally, it emerged in Ephesians 5.25 as a metaphor for the church's relationship with Christ, exhorting husbands to love their wives as Christ does the church.[5] The Patristic writer Origen established from the *Song of Songs* his theology of the superiority of spiritual love involving sexual renunciation.[6] Bernard of Clairvaux linked the bride of Christ image of mystical union with the relationship depicted in the *Song of Songs*. 'They are spouses now, and what other bond exists

---

[5] From the model that the husband is the head of the marriage as Christ is head of the church, it follows that wives submit to their husbands 'as if to the Lord' (Eph 5.22). Interestingly, Rosemary Ruether judges that the patriarchal nature of this image is used as a counterfoil to the social equality of celibacy: '[The writer] takes a symbol of the eschatological union of Christ and the Church, which is actually antithetical to human marriage and sexuality, and tries to impose it inappropriately on human marriage in order to counteract the tendencies of the early church to dissolve marriage into eschatological equality between celibate women and men'. Rosemary Radford Ruether, *Sexism and God-Talk: Towards a Feminist Theology*, Boston: Beacon, 1983, 141.

[6] Origen, *Homilies on the Song of Songs*, 1.2 and *passim*.

between spouses than that of mutual love?"[7] This image was developed by allegorising the *Song*'s lovers. The male prince was seen to be God. The bride, constantly yearning and searching for her beloved, was a figure of the human soul, or more specifically the celibate contemplative in search of deeper union with God.

For centuries celibates found in the profound imagery of this love poem a mystical understanding of their celibacy: Richard Rolle, Julian of Norwich, John of the Cross and Teresa of Avila. Yet all this mystical use of the *Song of Songs* involved hermeneutic contortions unacceptable to modern biblical criticism. These interpretations deny the essential meaning of this celebration of human love by allegorising the relationship and categorising it as marital love symbolising God's love of the human soul. The history of this spiritual interpretation of the *Song of Songs*[8] emphasises the extraordinary ingenuity involved in the appropriation of metaphor, so that sexual abstinence is found in its opposite, sexual experience.[9] At the basis of these spiritual interpretations is the moralistic presumption that the relationship celebrated in the *Song of Songs* is marriage. The nuptial image required little deciphering as it was a very visible sign, widely lived out in joy and suffering throughout society. It was easily appropriated to symbolise

7 St Bernard of Clairvaux, *On the Song of Songs*, Kalamazoo: Cistercian Publications, 1977, Sermon 83.3.
8 W.E. Phipps, The Plight of the Song of Songs, *Journal of American Academy of Religion*, March 1974, 82-100.
9 Margaret Miles describes this as 'symbolic of a firm sublimation of sexuality in Christianity'. Margaret Miles, *The Image and Practice of Holiness*, London: SCM Press, 1988, 154-5. But this spiritualised reinterpretation is not exclusively Christian having already begun in early Jewish hermeneutic that it is a midrash of Genesis 2-3, Marvin H. Pope, *Song of Songs*, NY: Anchor Bible, Doubleday, 1977, 208.

the unseen spiritual union sought by the religious celibate. Despite its inherent inappropriateness, the nuptial metaphor has richly sustained many celibates. It has also promoted the dualistic comparison of celibate and married lifestyles. The use of nuptial symbols in women's religious life emptied the metaphor's meaning by trivialising its form through contradiction.

> The use of bridal gowns and veils in reception and profession ceremonies, of marital euphemisms in the sections of rules and constitutions dealing with the vow of chastity, and of sentimental spousal language in spiritual literature, because it did not reflect the real experience of most religious, was seen as superficial at best and offensive at worst.[10]

Despite this history, there is value in exploring the *Song of Songs* for new understanding for a theology of celibacy. And this primarily because the persistence of the mystical union understanding of celibacy indicates it is integral to any restatement of the vow's meaning.

In the *Song of Songs* human sexuality and love is utterly celebrated, but the Hebrew scriptures' theological ease with such sensuous experience has not flowed over into the history of its Christian interpretation. Christianity has avoided the theological significance of a love poem that does not mention God yet revels in such sexual delight without mention of marriage and procreativity. The *Song* is fascinated by physical eroticism. The woman's attraction to her lover, the man's delight in the woman's movement and physique form the main subject matter (1.5-6,9-16; 2.1-3; 4.1-7,11-15; 5.10-16; 6.4-7; 7.2-10; 8.8-10). Physical

---

[10] Schneiders, *New Wineskins*, 116.

longing and intimacy are characteristic of their relationship. Its unusual mutuality and absence of male sexual dominance is contrasted with the brutality shown to the woman by the guards (5:7) and her conflict with the social convention that she must await her lover, not go seeking him (5:8). This rejection of gender-subordination translates sexual potency into joyful human respect, not self-gratification or repression. Their sexuality is not sacralised nor sublimated but one with the purpose of life. Despite its focus, it is not self-indulgent nor an escape from others, 'Neither escaping nor exploiting sex, they embrace and enjoy it.'[11] (1:3-4; 3:6-11; 5:8-9; 6:1,8-9; 8:13). The lovers are immersed in their community as much as each other so that 'the love between two welcomes the love and companionship of many'.[12]

There are environmental and cosmological allusions in the poem that point to a meaning beyond the personal relationship of two lovers. Alluding to Genesis 2-3, it indicates a relationship with the land and its creatures that was lost in paradise of Genesis. Love and YHWH are closely identified as interchangeable. Love is likened to that primeval order created out of chaos by the Creator. That 8.6b is the only possible echo of the name of YHWH in the poem is interesting support for this identification. For a Hebrew reader the association of YHWH with the creative power of love is more automatic than our use of language would imply. Commentators and theologians have struggled with the apparent absence of YHWH in the text. 'Though Yahweh is not mentioned by name, surely the

---

11   Phyllis Trible, *God and the Rhetoric of Sexuality*, 161.
12   Trible, 159.

divine Presence is in that erotic garden, else the dualistic alienations of sexism and spiritualism could not be so markedly transcended.'[13]

Much of the appropriation of the metaphor bride of Christ from the *Song of Songs* has exclusively focused on those poems that reveal the woman lover's desire for the beloved and her delight in his appearance. Celibates have also used the commitment texts at the end of the song (8.6-10) as a source for reflection and as a liturgical text for ceremonies that mark the various stages of profession of the vows. This selectivity misses the very physical and sensuous nature of the relationship between the lovers. Indeed, this selective domesticating of the wildness of the love worshipping in the *Song* has deprived the metaphor of its full humanity, and isolated the concept of celibacy from sexuality. Women's sexuality, so much celebrated in the *Song*, has been the greatest casualty of this censorship. Misappropriation of the *Song of Songs* is consistent with celibacy's traditional dualistic denial of human sexuality, particularly the good of women's sexuality. The *Song*'s celebration of women's sexuality is ignored, despite its centrality.

In 7.1-14 the dancing woman is described from her feet to her head. Every evocative device is called into use: movement, smell, taste, sight and touch. The erotic and genital are exalted. The captivating bare feet in sandals open the description then direct the reader toward the provocative, curving hips rotating in the style of a belly-dancer (7.2). The vulva, often inaccurately labelled 'the navel' by

---

[13] James B. Nelson, *Embodiment: An Approach to Sexuality and Christian Theology*, Minneapolis: Augsburg, 1978, 85.

anatomically prudish commentators[14], is the next focus. Likening her belly, the focal point of the dance, to a rounded heap of wheat has the double effect of recalling the suggestive nature of the dance and linking such delight in fertility with eschatological allusion to the agricultural prosperity of the reign of God (Ps 72:16).

Images that connect sex with power appear through the identification of the woman's body with geographical boundaries of the kingdom and likening her hair to power over monarchy: 'your hair is like draperies of purple; a king held captive in its tresses' (v. 6).[15] Refocusing on the vaginal area in vv. 9b-10,[16] the object of this admiration is declared, 'I belong to my lover and for me he yearns' (v. 11). This recalls the formula of mutual belonging that occurred at the opening of the *Song* in 2:16. This descriptive poem is a sensuous and intentional enjoyment of the sexual attributes of the woman. Its physicality and free suggestion of the purpose of all this admiration disallows any spiritualising of sexuality. Embodiment and human enjoyment are clearly the subject being explored in this poetry.

---

14 The vulva's logical position is in the sequence of the description after the thighs and before the abdomen. It is also unlikely that fluid secretion from a healthy navel would be admired. This prudishness crosses genders, e.g. Marcia Falk who euphemistically chooses 'hips' because she says: 'English has no word that is not either clinical or pornographic in tone', *Love Lyrics from the Bible: A Translation and Literary Study of the Song of Songs*, Sheffield: Almond, 1982, 127. Pope sees no such problem in using 'vulva', for 'the locus of the evermoist receptacle between the thighs and the belly would seem to favour the lower aperture' *Song of Songs*, 617-8. It is also likened to a wine bowl (v. 3), an allusion to the rounded vessel image of the sealed fountain at the centre of the enclosed garden metaphor for the woman in 4.12.
15 Purple being the colour exclusively worn by Eastern rulers until the end of the Roman Empire (*purpura regis*).
16 Not the face, because the preceding return reference to the breasts 'suggests some more distinctly feminine zone than the nose or mouth'. Pope, 636.

Commitment in 8:6-10 is expressed through unusually power-filled mood and language. Its tone is very eschatological: the immortality of love pointing to the new order of God. The seal could be a searing brand, denoting permanent branding, but the implication of ownership or slavery is negated in the poem's ending: 'Were one to offer all he owns to purchase love, he would be roundly mocked' (v.7b). The seal could also be a signet, sign jewellery, to be worn as protection, as a devotional talisman, or to recall the bestower. The image evokes love's strength and permanence even in face of death and the forces of disorder or chaos. This is consciously eschatological, a reversal of the fate of the lovers in the primordial Garden of Paradise of Genesis 2-3.

The theme of fidelity and permanence is sustained in the next poem vv. 8-10. The subject of the poem is the woman's physical readiness for marriage and her state of virginity. The poem leaves the ideal of paradise and returns to the realm of reality, of the political and economic position of women. Chastity is a commodity to be rewarded. Her violation is prevented by her being locked up, like any other threatened property. This contrasts with the idyllic security of the eschatological relationship in vv. 6-7. A world of ownership and violence exists alongside these lovers' union. The woman responds out of the confidence of her love.

> I am a wall,
> and my breasts are like towers.
> So now in his eyes I have become
> one to be welcomed. (v.10)

Her chastity is not only intact but she is also boldly free to announce her readiness for her lover. Love has survived the onslaught of the disorderly waters of the current social order as it did the primordial waters of chaos in Genesis. Chastity is a universal demand on women and a means of control over their lives. Societies that allow male sexual exploits outside married commitment are inevitably severe in punishing women whose virginity or chastity is doubted. The woman in this poem does not fail this social convention. She declares her chastity is not mere compliance with the obligations of being property, but rather her sexual choice as 'one producing peace' for her lover.[17] Again the *Song* reverses the gender-specific punishments implied in the divine punishment of Adam and Eve in Genesis 3, the woman sharing her lover's 'urge' rather than being subject to him. The mutuality of their relationship is conserved in the woman's sexual choice.

The theology of sexuality in the Song of Songs

Song of Songs' close identification of the creative and redeeming power of love with the creative and redeeming action of YHWH presents sexuality as collaborative with God. Love in the *Song of Songs* is expressed in embodied terms. It is not spiritual, in the sense that spiritual is defined in an other-worldly way over and against the physical nature of the human person. Rather, it is most physical, sensuous and public. The psychological attributes of the couple are not the focus of their praise and pleasure.

---

17 Pope's translation, 684-6. Both the use of the particle *k* (identifying the individual referred to with the common) and *salom* (a political as well as personal quality) indicate that the peace referred to in this is not merely localised to their relationship. It is also seen as an allusion to Jerusalem, city of peace.

Their bodily characteristics attract each other. Yet the poems exude this corporeal fascination within the boundaries and expression of the relationship. This relationship is sexual and committed, not profligate nor exclusive, neither 'platonic' nor promiscuous.

The love understood by the *Song of Songs* is for all, not a restrictive, exclusive relationship.[18] Its delight contrasts with the isolating fate of Adam and Eve in Genesis 3:16-19. Not only were the primeval pair excluded by gender differentiation from understanding each other's suffering, they also had the awful awareness that they contributed to each other's pain: Eve in her seduction of Adam, Adam in his domination of Eve.[19] The lovers in the *Song of Songs* experience love as an alternative to the negative experience of sexuality: those closed, obsessive, possessive, domineering, destructive, exploitative, violent, and repressed experiences of the other. The body-freedom of the *Song* is not merely personal, but a political statement of the possibility and desirability of sexual mutuality.

In the *Song of Songs* focus on the body emphasises a positive view of humanity at the same time as it alerts us to the responsibility that such a positive attitude requires. Love cannot survive selfish or oppressive intentions. The purpose of this love is to reveal God, embodied in love.[20] God is not a formal character or voice in these poems, but throughout the history of its interpretation God's presence

---

18   Pope, 162.
19   Trible, 160.
20   There is a significant connection between the attitude to the human body and one's ability to appreciate sacramentally. Sacramentality requires embodiment, hence the *Song*'s use of body easily conjures divine allusion: Mary Douglas, *Natural Symbols*, Harmondsworth: Penguin, 1973, 100,195.

has been constantly perceived. In 8:6-7 this purpose is proclaimed. Like YHWH, love is stronger than death and all the other powers of chaos. Love reveals God and God's saving action in the world.

A sexual metaphor for celibacy

This re-reading of the *Song of Songs* in order to reclaim its affective vision for a theology of celibacy indicates that it has universal themes that are appropriate for all human love. There is no exegetical evidence that it exclusively deals with marriage nor that it is purely a spiritual allegory of divine love. It displays three challenging elements for celibate loving.

The primary element is the body as the medium for expression, the image of creation and the essence of human creaturehood. With its celebration of the physical and sexual nature of humanity as inseparable from human personhood, the *Song* challenges the disembodied character of most theologies of celibacy. Through the denial of sexual passions, celibacy achieved a more spiritual human existence. A sexual understanding of salvation calls for a theology of celibacy that ceases such body-denial. Human sexuality and its desire for interrelatedness is another element of the bodily focus of the *Song*. Women's sexuality specifically is presented as good, as seeking mutual union instead of subordination, as not merely complementary to man's sexuality in some androgynous sense, but as delightful in itself and evocative of God's love. From this equality without absorption comes a third element, the non-dominating power of creative love. In the *Song* the power of the lovers is mutual and respectful. The death-defying power of love confronts the body-denying and love-denying inequalities of the power of domination. For too long the theology of celibacy has had an ecclesial political dominance over marriage, hierarchical ascendancy over lay Christian lifestyles, and destructively submitted women to a negative theology of their sexuality. The political implications for a theology of celibacy that is mutual, embodied and allows womanly understanding of human personhood are challenging and long overdue.

The Gospel of John

Another aspect of the mystical union metaphor of celibacy that was common before Vatican II is the symbol of the celibate as a dwelling place of the Holy Spirit (1 Cor 6:19-20). It symbolises a discipleship of exclusive dedication to a permanent posture of adoration, so integrated into the celibate's personhood that the celibate's body becomes the place of worship. It is particularly associated with virginity. This metaphor's expression of mystical union remained independent of the marital image of spouse of Christ and was more linked to a 'domesticated martyrdom', the sacrifice of self to God in a mystical identification with and interior assimilation to Christ.[21] Church Fathers like Isidore of Seville and Augustine saw virginity as a figure of the Church and its relationship to Christ in the consecration and total sacrifice of the person incorporated in the image of 'virginal temples'.[22]

---

21 Ignatius of Antioch, cited in S. Schneiders, Non-Marriage for the Sake of the Kingdom, 145-8.
22 Isidore, *De Ecclesiastics officiis* 2.c.18 (PL 83:804-5); Augustine, *Enarratio in Ps 147,10* (PL 37, 1920).

These concepts of consecration and sacrifice have provided celibates with a more interiorised image of their relationship with Christ. While the term 'Temple of the Holy Spirit' is seldom directly used, it is this concept that underlies most presentations of mystical union with Christ.[23] Recent Papal teaching emphasises the 'special' nature of this union. This is reflected in descriptions like: 'sacred consecration', 'consecrated in a more total way', 'mutual loving presence between God and ourselves', and 'keeping a vigil of love' to cite a few.[24] Some recent writers are critical that the metaphor's 'reduction of the essence of religious celibacy to nothing more than a special relationship of solitude with God has often led to excessive individualism and to an overly spiritualistic, and therefore deficient understanding of religious celibacy'.[25] This metaphor fails to avoid the association of celibacy with an other-worldliness that is both superior and privatistic.

The Pauline uses of the temple metaphor are soteriological and ecclesial, indicating that true discipleship of Christ disallows any need for ritual purification or any other pantheistic 'insurance'-type worship (1 Cor 3:16-19, 6:19; 2 Cor 6:16). These texts are not concerned therefore with the nature of God's indwelling in the individual or the community of faith, but with the power of Christian salvation over other religious practices and beliefs. There is

---

23 An exception being T. Dubay, Virginal Temples, *Review for Religious* 27, 1968, 21-43.
24 Respectively: R. Faricy, *The End of the Religious Life*, Minneapolis: Winston, 1983, 40-41; Pope John Paul II, *Essential Elements* II,1,14; R. Egenter, Virginity: Some Ethical and Ascetical Aspects, A. Auer et al., *Celibacy and Virginity*, Dublin: Gill & Son, 1968, 105.
25 G.A. Aschenbrenner, Celibacy in Community and Ministry, *Human Development* 6, $985, 27.

not any direct association of the metaphor here with celibacy, except perhaps their proximity to the references to celibacy in 1 Corinthians 6:19 with 1 Corinthians 7.

The application of the temple of the Holy Spirit as a metaphor for celibacy has not been drawn specifically from this Pauline theology. Similarly, celibacy is not at all the interest of the Johannine use of indwelling as a metaphor for discipleship. As represented in John, indwelling is a more dynamic image of the Christian life. It resists a single meaning for mystical union, like marriage, as in bride of Christ, or like an ecclesial or cultic dedication, as in temple.

Indwelling recurs frequently throughout John's Gospel. It describes the union of the Father and Christ, the relationship of true believers to Christ, and the interrelationship between believers. 'To abide/indwell' and its Greek cognates 'to be in', 'to remain', 'to inhabit' appear over forty times in the Gospel of John, compared with a total of twelve times in the Synoptic Gospels. There appears to be a structural pattern in the recurrence of the revelatory '*I am*' statements, in Jesus' significant encounters with women, and these indwelling texts. The juxtaposition of these provides an unusual prominence to women's experience in the Gospel's drama of the revelation and glorification of Christ.

The commentators are clearer about what indwelling is not, than what it is. Dodd and Brown claim that it is not personal inclusion nor absorption into the godhead or divine being in a pantheistic sense. Nor is it like divine inhabiting of a temple or other sacred structure, nor an ecstatic possession as in mysticism or demonic possession. Dodd describes 'indwelling' as 'the sharing in one life', as 'nothing so external as mere obedience or imitation', as 'the most intimate union conceivable between God and man.'[26]

In the Prologue, specifically 1:13 and 1:18, indwelling is associated with birth. 'Who were born not of blood, nor of the will of the flesh, nor of the will of man, but of the will of God.' Indwelling is presented as a metaphor for the Johannine understanding of 'justification' in 1:13. Here the efficacy of ritual sacrifice ('not of blood'), worship, penance and prayers ('nor of the will of flesh'), even good deeds and lives ('nor of the will of humans') are all superseded by that intimate reciprocal indwelling that is being 'born of God'. 'No-one has ever seen God, the only Son who is in the bosom (womb) of the Father, he has made him known' (v. 18). This introduces the term 'bosom' or 'womb' as an attribute of God the Father, an allusion to the uterus and the indwelling of pregnancy.[27] Schneiders sees this text as one of the clearest New Testament images of the femininity of God.[28]

Another use of indwelling is as an image of salvation in the discussion with Nicodemus in 3:3-9. Jesus responds to Nicodemus' query about the source of his authority: 'unless one is born anew he cannot enter the kingdom of God' and 'unless one is born again of water and the spirit, he cannot enter the kingdom of God'. Here entry into the

---

26 C.H. Dodd, *The Interpretation of the Fourth Gospel*, Cambridge: C.U.P., 1953, 197.
27 'womb' as *kólpos* appears in medical and poetic references from the 5th century BCE to the 2nd century CE: H.D. Liddell and R. Scott, *Greek-English Lexicon*, Oxford: O.U.P., 1966, 974; E.A. Sophocles, *Greek Lexicon of the Roman and Byzantine Periods from 146 BC to AD 1100*, NY: Ungar, 1957, 676.
28 'We are, in John's Gospel, *tekna theou* children engendered by the God who is both Jesus' Father and our Father (cf. 1.13).' Sandra Schneiders, Born Anew, *Theology Today* 44, 1987, 194.

kingdom of God is associated with rebirth through the womb. When Nicodemus expresses alarm about being 'born again', Jesus insists on the physical nature of his metaphor. He is not speaking spiritually here because in 3:12 he admonishes Nicodemus' unbelief with the declaration: 'If I have told you earthly things and you do not believe, how can you believe if I tell you heavenly things?' Only then does he begin referring to the heavenly things, through to v. 21. Jesus is emphatically physical in this analogy, speaking 'metaphorically but concretely'.[29] The Johannine community again alludes to physical birth in the images of water and spirit. A pregnant woman's water breaks just prior to the labour of birth, and spirit refers to life, as in 19:30.[30] Physical birth is used as a Johannine image for salvation, salvation through the uterus of God.

The indwelling nature of these unifying relationships continues to be physically couched in that closest biological form of union, pregnancy – union within the uterus.[31] According to Brown, 'it is the reciprocal in-dwelling – an

---

29 One of Brueggemann's 'tasks of the prophetic imagination', *The Prophetic Imagination*, Philadelphia: Fortress, 1978, 50.
30 Schneiders detects here two types of birth: 'human birth of flesh from flesh' hence the breaking of waters, and 'spiritual birth of spirit from spirit': Born Anew, 192. But this seems to be a premature movement into the spiritual that does not account for the distinction in 3:12, despite her recognition that *there* is 'the literal meaning of Jesus' discourse', 193. It would appear more feasible to link the water and spirit with physical birth in order to avoid the separate association of 'water' with chaos, a confusing and a possibly blasphemous denigration to being 'born anew'.
31 The pregnancy image of John 1:21, while not unique in scripture, is developed differently from other related texts. There are Old Testament analogies to the conclusion of pregnancies in Isaiah 26:16-19 and 66:7-14. These inadequately explain the meaning of this passage: Isaiah 26 depicts a 'phantom pregnancy', only wind, which ends in anti-climax, not a hope-giving expectation of life; Isaiah 66 is a premature birth.

intimate union, something dynamic, not static'.[32] This is epitomised in the pivotal passage of the Last Supper discourses.

> When a woman is in travail she has sorrow, because her hour has come. But when she is delivered of the child she no longer remembers the distress for the joy that a human being is born into the world (16:21).[33]

This image of the birth process can therefore be seen as a parallel to the death and resurrection of Jesus. Only through Christ's coming into the world could the disciples be enabled to indwell/abide with God.[34] Since the exaltation on the cross is the high-point of the Johannine Jesus' mission to the world, this comparison of the exaltation with pregnancy is remarkable. Using an exclusively woman's experience is an unusual association. It promotes pregnancy and, by implication, the value of women's sexuality.

For first century Palestinian society this association of pregnancy and the exaltation of the Saviour is shocking. In the religious practice of Jewish society, the time after birth is the period of uncleanness, yet this is the sign of the imminent kingdom of God. Such a scandalous likening

---

32 R. Brown, *The Gospel According to John* vol 1, London: Anchor Bible, Chapman, 1966, 510-11.
33 In his analysis of the discourse of 13:1-17:26, Moloney sees this passage in chiasmic parallel to 14:15-24, where the subject is the mutual indwelling that results from love. F. Moloney, *Woman: First Among the Faithful*, Melbourne: Dove, 1985, 83-5.
34 Schnackenburg finds that this text 'gives the disciples an active part in the birth of the messiah (or the exaltation of Jesus)'. R. Schnackenberg, *The Gospel According to St John* vol 3, NT: Crossroad, 1982, 158; Elisabeth Schussler-Fiorenza understands that in this text 'the Johannine Jesus likened the hour of his exaltation on the cross and the time of the disciples' bereavement to the experience a pregnant woman has before and after giving birth', *In Memory of Her*, London: SCM, 1983, 325.

of cultic impurity with Christ must indicate something very important and powerful for the Johannine community to risk its offence and scandalous misunderstanding. As the use of human being and the child in 16:21 are gender-inclusive, the contemporary cultural practice of no joy at the birth of a female is challenged. This indicates a significant break with the traditional attitude towards women and a radical identification and integration of women into full discipleship, even to the degree of deeming their gender's experience fit to be metaphor for the exaltation of Christ and the coming of the kingdom of God.

Discipleship in the Johannine community is understood as that 'indwelling' relationship which is a sharing in the intimate union of the Father and Jesus. The emphasis on women in the Gospel neither discounts males nor elevates women to an idealised type. Mutual indwelling is presented as the primary criterion for the disciple's union with Christ. Biological determinism is avoided. The metaphor avoids gender exclusion by recalling that all humans share in the experience of once having dwelt in the womb. The metaphor shows indwelling with Christ as available to all humanity. It is this gender-inclusive discipleship and the equality of woman believers that contrasts the Johannine community with other Christian communities.[35]

---

35 R.E. Brown, Roles of Women in the Fourth Gospel, *Woman: New Dimensions*, W.J. Burghardt ed., (NY: Paulist, 1975, 113-125, *The Community of the Beloved Disciple*, London: Chapman, 1974, 94, and *The Churches the Apostles Left Behind*, NY: Paulist, 1984, 94-5; Sandra M. Schneiders, Women in the Fourth Gospel and the Role of Women in the Contemporary Church, *Biblical Theology Bulletin XII, 1982, 35-45*.

A theology of indwelling

The image of mystical union is developed by the Johannine metaphor into an interactive, more organic experience of intimate being. Not a place to be found, a worship to be performed, nor an ethic to be imitated, the metaphor signals that indwelling is neither alienable nor dependent on the efforts of the disciples. The relationship between a pregnant woman and the offspring forming in her uterus is the model for the organic unity between Christ and his disciples. It is a womanly sign because of the gender-specificity of pregnancy, but it is also an inclusive sign, because all humans have experienced the intimate union of foetal development in the uterus. Indwelling is therefore an incarnate sign of inclusive union, of its availability to all, and of the value of female humanity and sexuality from whom the metaphor is derived.

Despite the tendency to value office and ministry/charism in the Pastorals and other New Testament writings, John's Gospel emphasises that only indwelling discipleship is important. This emphasis counters discrimination against women since the beginning of the churches.[36] This indwelling discipleship is open to all believers and to all those to whom they are sent in the world (17:18). The organic, inclusive and relational nature of such discipleship and union with Christ also resists hierarchies of merit. It is inclusion in God that is sought, not salvation through any human efforts. Its mission is service of one another, 'intercarnating' the indwelling experience of union. It also throws into question any attempt to justify theologically

---

36 R.E. Brown, *The Churches the Apostles Left Behind*, 94.

sexual renunciation as necessary for fuller discipleship. The sign of uterine indwelling is a sign to all believers to seek union with their God in a relational way, that allows themselves to abide in love. This sign allows for difference and co-existence. Otherwise, like the androcentric fallacies of male 'imago Christi' arguments,[37] only pregnant women (not post-partum females, pre-pubiles, sterile females, virgins, males, etc.) would be saved.

An indwelling metaphor for celibacy

Celibacy is not a concern for the Johannine community. To the Gospel community a woman in childbirth is the eschatological sign, not celibacy as traditionally assumed by the Church. While the sign is pregnancy, to mistake its signal as defining the limits of the meaning of union with Christ is to idolise the sign. The organic, inclusive and relational nature of union with Christ exceeds all boundaries of human experience. What is asserted in the sign is the intimate experience of that union, indwelling, a positive valuing of women's sexuality. The Johannine metaphor incarnates the desire for union with Christ. It is not a cerebral or disembodied union, but one which calls for the holistic expression of union beyond either ritual or ethical purity.

To assert the sign-value of women's sexuality does not automatically dismiss the validity of women's celibacy. It demands that women's celibacy be expressed in terms other

---

[37] Pontifical Biblical Commission, Can Women be Priests', *Origins* 6, 1976, 92-26; Sacred Congregation for the Doctrine of the Faith, Vatican Declaration: Women in the Ministerial Priesthood, *Origins* 6, 1977, 517-524.

than those which deny women's sexuality. The indwelling is sexual but does not limit union to coitus or pregnancy. An exclusive over-identification with the image counteracts the very inclusiveness and diversity that this metaphor offers.[38] Women's freedom from oppression and exclusion is part of the kingdom's inclusive program (cf John 8:3-11).

In contrast biological determinism, the experience of infertility as failure, oppressive relationships, and fear of loss continue to prevent women from full realisation of their salvation. Celibacy allows religious women to assume control over their own bodies, in a way which is different to denying their sexuality in order to maintain control or be controlled.[39] There is human creativity beyond childbearing. Interpersonal ownership is not the only way to commit oneself to others. Can there be free embodiment of the absence of partners and childlessness? The Johannine values of organic, inclusive and relational indwelling provide transforming criteria for celibate women to discriminate between the Kingdom-like freedom in assuming control of their bodies and the bondage of body denial and selfishness. The society of discipleship created by the intercarnation of human experience of God in John's Gospel, reveals the need for more serious re-viewing of the embodied, womanly and sociological elements of celibacy.

---

[38] 'For women as well as men, use of the childbirth metaphor is psychologically charged and over-determined. But while men's use of the metaphor begins in a fascination for the Other, women's use originates in conflict with themselves as other.' Susan S. Friedman, Creativity and the Childbirth Metaphor: Gender Difference in Literary Discourse, *Feminist Studies* 13, 1987, 65.

[39] 'Women's oppression begins with the control of the body, the fruits of labor.' *Ibid.*, 70.

The Prophet Jeremiah

Vatican II demanded a new consciousness of the world and its needs in the heightened political consciousness of the nineteen-sixties. Consequently many religious men and women found in the figure of the prophet an alternative image for religious life to spousal union. This notion of prophecy in the religious life was derived from a general sense of the prophetic tradition rather than from any specific focus on the celibate prophet Jeremiah. Also celibacy was not particularly described as a prophetic activity in this writing. The vows of poverty and obedience and the service nature of the apostolic life were described more as prophetic.[40] Very few writers allude to the celibate sign in Jeremiah 16 as a source for the theology of celibacy.[41] The absence of direct reference to Jeremiah's celibacy is not so surprising given its marginal interest for the largely Protestant scholarship on Jeremiah. Despite this, the prophetic election of Jeremiah by YHWH (1:4-10), his second call (15:10-21), and the new covenant material in Jeremiah (31:31-34) are frequently referred to in general writing on the vowed life.

Jeremiah's celibacy is a unique sign in the Old Testament.[42] Israel emphasises the divine obligation to produce

---

40 This prophetic character of religious life was not exclusively claimed for apostolic religious life. Thomas Merton's seminal and influential writings on the relevance of contemplative religious life make the same claim. Cf. *Contemplation in a World of Action*, NY: Doubleday, 1965.
41 'It is not evident that for Jeremiah celibacy was a state of consecrated life. However by God's order he became a *sign* for the people.' L. Laberge, Celibacy in the Bible, *Consecrated Celibacy*, Donum Dei 16, Ottawa: Canadian Religious Conference, 1971, 15.
42 Except for Judith's celibacy assumed in widowhood (Judith 16:22), and references to temporary celibacy for a divine mission.

male offspring from faithful marriage. Unmarried and childless lives bore the sign of YHWH's disfavour. The very offence of Jeremiah's condition guaranteed that the extraordinary meaning of the sign would be heard, even if not heeded. The centrality of marriage to the order of Jewish life made it an accessible image for the prophetic call to religious and social faithfulness. This marital image was unambiguous and understandable because it likened faithfulness to the covenant with God to the evident social and economic importance of faithful marriage.[43] This was essential as the prophet's purpose depended on his audience understanding his proclamation.

Many of the sisters interviewed personally identified with this metaphor of the prophetic sign. Yet the conflation of this metaphor with an eschatological apocalyptic world-renunciation, and the absence of specific anchoring of the metaphor to any prophetic source, calls for a more deliberate re-reading of the Jeremiah texts for their illumination of celibacy as a prophetic sign.

The difficulties of the prophet's role are a major concern of the Book of Jeremiah. Jeremiah's opposition-ridden mission and his sufferings represent a shift in the prophetic role: 'in Jeremiah all the forms of expression to be found in classical prophecy are obviously breaking up'.[44] Jeremiah's prophetic awareness sensed the social and ecological pollution of sin as total in a way only lately

---

[43] This is particularly evident in the prophet Hosea where infidelity is used as the counter-covenant image — a 'pornographic' appropriation and objectification of women as seen by T. Drorah Setel, Prophets and Pornography; Female Sexual Imagery in Hosea, *Feminist Interpretation of the Bible*, L. Russell ed., Oxford: Blackwell, 1985, 86-95.

[44] G. Von Rad, *The Message of the Prophets*, London: SCM Press, 1968, 162.

recognised by modern environmental concern. War's destruction is cited in 4:5-21; 6:1-5, 22-26; 20:4-6; land devastation in 9:9-10; 12:9-13; 14:2-6; 17:5; 18:16; disintegration of social relationships in 3:33-34; 9:16-21; 15:7-9; 19:7-9. 'In Jeremiah we are conscious of a prophet's feeling of solidarity with his people in their danger, and even with the land itself in hers, such as we shall never meet with again.'[45]

Jeremiah's accusation that YHWH is unfaithful to his prophet in chapter 15 is very significant. It immediately succeeds two communal laments by the people (14:2-9 and 14:17-22). In these, the people claim they are repenting in response to his announcement of judgment. They desire to avoid this judgment and promise to return to faithful observance of their covenant with YHWH. Jeremiah has apparently achieved his prophetic task. Suddenly YHWH refuses to accept this response. YHWH appears to renege on the deal. Exasperated, Jeremiah wants to quit.[46] As with his judgment on the people, YHWH refuses to comfort Jeremiah. Jeremiah's prophetic role has to change. He must now share with YHWH the suffering of the people's rejection. Jeremiah's rebellion lay in his unwillingness to share in YHWH's suffering. He has not recognised the seriousness of the people's dislocation from YHWH.

Jeremiah is commanded by YHWH to be celibate (16:1-4). Marrying and having children no longer assures the future, these offspring will also be obliterated. Hence YHWH's command is to choose what is inevitable, to

---

45 Von Rad, 165.
46 The Exilic editors were also astounded by this turnabout so here they inserted a prose addition (14:11-16) that attempts to 'explain' or soften YHWH's reversal.

announce concretely through his celibacy the de-generation that is the whole community's fate. Jeremiah's celibacy is as public and communal as it is personal. Eschewing marriage and children just as YHWH experiences the relinquishing of the covenant relationship and its fruitfulness, Jeremiah's celibacy means an end to his generativity, his personal future and his biological and social contribution to the future of his community. In this condition he shares the destructive future Judah has chosen for itself by its rebellion. 'The sense of being part of a chain between past and future was so strong that one must understand Jeremiah to be called to extinction as an act symbolic of YHWH's decision for the nation.'[47]

This is underscored by the prohibition against celebrating funerals and weddings (vv. 8-9). Self-chosen extinction is neither a death nor a new life to be celebrated. The denial of marriage silences 'the sounds of joy and gladness' (v. 9). Through this celibacy the prophet must live out fully the consequences of the rebellion of YHWH's people, 'by his life he should symbolize the death of his people'.[48] As McKane comments, 'when the sounds of wedding festivities are no longer heard, death is overtaking life, for a community with a future is one in which new homes are always being made and children continue to be born'.[49]

---

[47] W.L. Holladay, *Jeremiah 1*, Philadelphia: Hermeneia Commentary, Fortress, 1986, 469.
[48] Holladay, 469; cf. also W. McKane, *Jeremiah* vol 1, Edinburgh: T. & T. Clark, 1986, 367.
[49] McKane, 367. Also Gary Anderson, Celibacy or Consummation in the Garden, *Harvard Theological Review* 82, 1898, 136: 'In the sixth blessing [of marriage], the imagery of Jeremiah is used. He had characterized the era of mourning, or divine curse which was to follow the destruction of the Temple and land, as a time when the sounds of mirth and joy, of bridegroom and bride would cease from the cities of Judah and the streets

This echoes the hopeless mourning of the mother of seven in 15:9, 'gasping out her life; her sun sets in full day'. By allusion it is a figure of YHWH as parent of the seven tribes of Israel/Judah also suffering the effects of their extinction. The celibacy enjoined on Jeremiah is therefore a sign on many levels. It symbolises Jeremiah's prophetic proclamation, his identification with the fate of the community, the environmental effects of Judah's rebellion against the Creator of the universe, the lost future for the community, the severe change of his prophetic role, and the suffering of YHWH.

Celibacy is presented as a prophetic sign of both the extremity of the destruction caused by rebellion and how YHWH can hold out a future for his rebellious community even though all the indications are that their life is at an end. It is such a culturally contradictory sign from YHWH because non-marriage and lack of child-bearing were so offensive to the community. Therein lies its potency. It is like Jeremiah's outrageous symbolic actions of broken, misused, decaying and wasted things, but it is far more startling. Lack of generativity was clearly a punishment from YHWH (particularly on women). Here YHWH demands that his prophet wear this sign of punishment as a message of YHWH's future action.[50] Like parable, it

---

of Jerusalem (Jer 7:34; 16:9, 25:6). By contrast the era of restoration would be characterized by the return of these joyful signs (Jer 33:10-11). So also the sixth benediction characterizes the end times as one of marital joy'.

50 There appears to be little reference to male impotence and use of it metaphorically in the Jewish tradition (perhaps due to the patriarchal supposition that all males are fertile and the exclusive biological source of life and that infertility comes only from women's failure to be procreative). Several traditions of Midrash see in the barren woman 'a sign of the world to come'. Cf. A. Brenner, *The Israelite Woman: Social Role and Literary Type in Biblical Narrative*, Sheffield: JSOT, 1985, 135.

reverses the natural order of things, the expected consequences, the way things usually happen. The rejection of the natural course of marriage and child-bearing becomes not only a sign of death and the pre-eschatological era of mourning but a pre-figuration of the hope in YHWH's intervention at some future time.

Thus this prophet experiences a severe dislocation from the security of his past and is drawn into a different order of eschatological dimension, the new order of YHWH's time. The prophetic sign, unlike other oracles, becomes eschatological, less immediate in its fulfilment. The prophetic sign of celibacy particularly indicates this shift. It witnesses to a fulfilment well beyond the prophet's life, both in time and essence. The prophet cannot enjoy the security of creating a future for his descendants. His life and future ends in order to witness to the future of the community.

Jeremiah's celibacy is also a sign of the current and imminent destruction of Judah, its inhabitants, its cities, its land. His lack of generativity indicates the full tragedy of the community's sin and its consequences. Jeremiah embodies the desolation of the environment, the hopelessness of relationships, the isolation and loneliness of being friendless among enemies, the pathos of the self-destructing community. In this sign he signals, in his own extinction, the real horror. Jeremiah's celibacy has communal consequences, just as his prophetic vocation called him out of private and personal existence into a public and communal responsibility.

A theology of prophetic sign

Jeremiah's celibacy is an apt source from which to construct a theology of celibacy. This celibacy is a sign from YHWH of the destruction and lack of social generativity that result from sin and rebellion. It is also an ecological sign that indicates the connectedness of creation by showing that disorder and pollution in personal, religious and social life adversely affect all life.[51] It is also a sign for the sign-bearer, the prophet. It emphasises the prophet's new call by more radically identifying the sign-bearer with the fate the sign is pointing towards. The celibate prophet already lives out (prefigures) the de-generative fate of the people and the land. By such a public sign the personal deprivation of a private fate becomes an offensive political challenge to the community. Celibacy totally dissolves the distinction between public and private, personal and communal, even human and cosmic. This celibacy is a radical sign of human responsibility and the illegitimacy of dualistic demarcation.

The purpose of this sign is to point out the lack of generativity that results from the breaking of the covenant between the Creator and the created. This de-generation affects the relationship of the covenant, prevents the traditional means of salvation from being implemented, and pushes out to an unknown future any hope of restoration of the relationship. This degeneration has universal effects. The Creator is prevented from acting for this people and

---

[51] This concept of the interrelatedness of microcosmic and macrocosmic pollution has extensive representation in the literature of the ancient world and in other biblical sources besides Jeremiah, e.g. Ps 107:33-34; Isaiah 24:4-13; Micah 6:12-16; Hosea 4:1-3; Joel 1:8-12; Amos 4:6-10; Zephaniah 2:.8-9; Job 38:22-30.

the creation. The people are unable to reform themselves and to form new life. The prophet is unable to mediate and proclaim a message of hope. The land is unable to be fertile. The sign also indicates the human responsibility for all this destruction. The prophet's celibacy, a voluntary form of extinction, appears irresponsible in relation to the future, but much more was the people's rebellion irresponsible about its future consequences.

A prophetic metaphor for celibacy

Jeremiah's celibacy and its context offer interesting insight into the prophetic role and meaning of celibacy today. Today's ecological destruction caused by human industrial and agricultural exploitation of the environment is like the environmental consequences of Judah's rebellion. Socially, economically and politically, we feel the effects of our ecological arrogance. Our sinfulness not only includes personal and social destruction of other humans through war, violence and oppression of all kinds, but also the destruction of our world and its ability to sustain life in the future. Our generativity is threatened by the extinction of other species, ecosystem destruction and climate disorder. All these are the consequences of our sinful rebellion against the created world.

The celibate's lack of generativity is like the imminent fate of all creation. It also signals that the loneliness and isolation of the celibate are small compared with the more pervasive personal and social suffering caused by the arrogant and violent oppression of others. Even when people begin to regret the disorder they wreak, the previous order cannot be restored. The old ways of solving things, supplanting one exploitative system with another, are no longer effective. The celibate prophet is called to share in the suffering of the Creator and the creation. The celibate personally, bodily suffers the lack of generativity, voluntarily overseeing her own extinction, as a sign of the severity of the disorder of life, its destruction and suffering. Such voluntary extinction would be merely irresponsible were it not also a witness to a future hope. The sign-value of the celibate, in terms of Jeremiah's prophetic celibacy, lies in her ability to communicate the immediate and impending horror, through the offence of being celibate. Only then can the need for a future be proclaimed adequately.[52]

There is an ecological dimension to this prophetic sign, that involves seeing the connectedness of created things, proclaiming human interrelationship with all creation and our responsibility for the creation. A future orientation in this sign delivers it from being merely a 'woe' proclamation to become an eschatological witness to a promise yet to be fulfilled. This refuses the magic solutions of 'instant' culture, the latest in consumer 'religious' solutions, to save one's world.

The sign of celibacy is not a solution. Its offence is that it points to the need for a solution beyond the traditional expectations and sources. It indicates who is in control of the future and of our future generativity. It reveals that God activates the fulfilment of the promise. To risk a tautology, as a true sign it points to something beyond itself.

---

52 Brueggemann lists one of the tasks of 'prophetic imagination' as: 'to speak metaphorically but concretely about the real deathliness that hovers over us and gnaws within us, and to speak neither in rage nor in cheap grace, but with the candor born of anguish and passion'. *The Prophetic Imagination*, 50.

New metaphors for women's celibacy

An indication of the resilience of metaphors and the metaphorical nature of these biblical sources is that they have continued communicating something of the diversity of religious celibate living without ever formally defining it. Re-reading the scriptural sources for the traditional metaphors reveals such a surplus of meanings that, instead of these images freezing the variety of our understanding, they actually function to invite our suspicion of undisclosed possibilities for understanding celibacy through them. Metaphor by its nature refuses to be complete, systematic and refined. It has therefore been an appropriate vehicle for the preservation of the diversity of reflection on the experience of celibacy. Because metaphor is inappropriate use of meaning outside of its context,[53] the preservation of any meaning through metaphor refuses any one absolute definition. Sallie McFague observes that 'imagistic language does not just tolerate interpretation but demands it'.[54]

Metaphor does not equal theology. Therefore we must be aware of not trying to force these metaphors into use beyond their limitations. Careful examination of surplus meanings in these sources offers a new theological way of interpreting celibacy. Despite the distance between the metaphor and its source, the metaphorical dynamic ensured that this tension would ever be evident, inviting suspicion and awaiting discovery.

From this re-reading of the scriptural sources for the traditional metaphors used to describe and understand

---

53 Sallie McFague, *Models of God*, London: SCM Press, 1987, 33.
54 McFague, *Metaphorical Theology*, Philadelphia: Fortress, 1982, 22.

celibacy emerge three elements for a theological reconstruction of celibacy that incorporates women's experience. These are:

(1) the body as integral to any human understanding and the inseparability of human sexuality from human personhood;

(2) woman as a significant referent for a full understanding of the incarnation and the inter-carnation of Christian discipleship and community; and

(3) the prophetic significance of signalling the connectedness of all created things, of human relations, and of creaturehood and the Creator.

These elements provide useful starting-points and a means for theologising on the experience of celibacy. The body represents a metaphorical shift from privatistic sexual experience of the other to political and public commitment to the other. It identifies the use of sexual power in private and public relationships. As a result, the body becomes the starting-point for understanding the power and politics of celibacy. Acknowledging women's experience relocates theology away from universal absolutes to more gender-inclusive awareness. The meaning of celibacy would be enhanced by the different theological perspective of a woman's socio-theology. Finally, the role of the sign and its incompleteness, its inter-connection with what it signifies, opens up an ecological theological perspective on celibacy. These biblical sources withdraw any biblical authority for the maintenance of a dualistic theology of celibacy. Rather, they emphasise the need to imbue any theology of celibacy with an embodied attitude towards human sexuality, with a serious incorporation of the experience of women, and a thoroughgoing awareness that celibacy's responsibility extends beyond an anthropocentric focus.

3

Sexuality and women's celibacy

> *'A nun's life – free as a bird.*
> *A nun – a door unopened.'*
> Kassia (9th century Byzantine Greek Nun)[1]

A world-view that sees the spiritual realm opposed to matter and the world defines human sexuality and women's sexuality, in particular, as something negative and needing to be controlled. Sexuality is equated with the disorder and destruction of chaos. Yet as Margaret Farley suggests:

> There is growing general evidence that sex is neither the indomitable drive that early Christians thought it was nor the primordial impulse of early psychoanalytic theory. When it was culturally repressed, it seemed an inexhaustible power, underlying other motivations, always struggling to express itself in one way or another. Now that it is less repressed, more and more free and in the open, it is easier to see other complex motivations behind it,

---

[1] Kassia, in Carol Cosman et al., *The Penguin Book of Women Poets*, Harmondsworth: Penguin, 1979.

and to recognize its inability in and of itself to satisfy the affective yearning of persons.[2]

The folly of dualism is that its emphasis on opposites inadvertently promotes what it is trying to oppose. When the physicality of sex is curbed: 'The man who is enjoined to abstinence is being both encouraged and discouraged at the same time; sexual tension is being augmented by giving to sex an enhanced psychic value'.[3] In contrast the love relationship of the *Song of Songs* declares human sexuality to be good, as the creation is good, because it embodies love like the creation embodies the Creator's love. God prefers working through not against creation. Human sexuality is promoted as integral to this creation, just as it is integral to the lovers' relationship. The negative dualistic attitude to human sexuality denies that 'our human sexuality is God's good gift. It is fundamental to our created and our intended humanness'.[4] Equally, it denies 'the confidence that our Creator has so designed the self's erotic dynamism that it is intrinsically aimed not at impersonal sexual hedonism but at personal sexual communion'.[5] The risk of dualism is to divide God against Godself. Such dualism errs in its tacit declaration that God is not in control.

Embodied celibacy

Traditionally celibacy is presented as loving commitment of the whole person to God and loving service of all

---

[2] Margaret Farley, An Ethic for Same Sex Relations, in R.A. Nugent (ed.), *Challenge to Love*, New York: Crossroad, 1987, 103.
[3] Germaine Greer, *Sex and Destiny*, London; Picador, 1984, 89.
[4] Nelson, 272.
[5] Nelson, 86.

humanity. The faith implied in these ideals is that God loves humanity and demonstrates that love by calling particular persons to evidence that love through focusing their life and their ministry on the service of others who are not especially related to them. As God created humans as sexual beings, it would appear counter-creational to require some humans not to employ their sexuality, as a sign of God's love for humanity.

A negative view of sexuality is not consistent with faith in creation. Rather, it is connected more to unredeemed fears of death and anger.[6] A celibacy that represses sexuality risks disembodiment thereby becoming a caricature of God's creativity, because it confuses relinquishing of sexual procreativity and genital intimacy with an angelic existence. To be sexual is essential to human nature. A disembodied celibacy can only be abstract and a celibacy of the mind. Sexuality is more than genital activity, 'it is who we *are* as body-selves who experience the emotional, cognitive, physical, and spiritual need for intimate communion − human and divine'.[7]

Celibacy does not require a destruction of sexuality. It is as much about 'what it means that we as body-selves participate in the reality of God, and as body-selves reflect upon − theologise about − that reality' as other sexually

---

[6] 'Underneath this fear of embodiment as moral debasement lies the fear of death.' Rosemary Ruether, *To Change the World*, London: SCM Press, 1981, 61; 'Klein suggests that the guilt and shame around sexuality are cloaks for another emotion − anger − specifically, anger with parents.' Naomi Goldenberg, Archetypal Theory and the Separation of Mind and Body: Reason Enough to Turn to Freud, *Journal of Feminist Studies in Religion* 1, 1985, 71.

[7] Nelson, 86.

active human lifestyles.[8] About her sexuality one sister observed:

> 'Sexuality is broader than the genital aspect of sexual relations it is something about my whole person, my relationships, my expressing myself in all sorts of ways. My understanding of my sexuality has been broadened and deepened through these relationships. Because I've made a commitment to be celibate it means that I've had to make some choices about the way I've entered into those relationships.' (44)

Celibacy is always defined as not sexual, rather than as a different experience of human sexuality.[9] To be celibate requires a consciousness of sexuality rather than a denial of it, as another sister claims:

> 'That there are celibates around helps the quality of life. In that one is more conscious of one's relationships and more intentional and more caring, because you're not getting pulled into something like lotus land, where your flesh makes you forget the wholeness of your being. For me celibacy is more intentional.' (48)

The traditional understanding sought in celibacy was a union with God that was mediated other than in human partnership. A sexually embodied celibacy would experience the search for unity with the divine as total, including the whole person and all her interpersonal experiences. This cannot preclude being sexual. The sexuality and relationships of celibates are the embodiment of their communion with God, not distractions or temptations from it.

---

8   Nelson, 20.
9   Anne Wilson Schaef identifies the lack of a 'theology of differences' as an ideological support for the myth 'that *the White Male System is the only thing that exists*'. *Women's Reality*, San Francisco: Harper and Row, 1981, 8.

> 'It is not a question of celibate or married, but simply one of finding God's will for each of his creatures, whether it be plant, animal or human. If we live as he would wish us to, the Kingdom does come and is visible.' (69)

> 'If I am to be a fulfilled woman, who is aware of and committed to Jesus and humankind, I need to be in touch with what is happening in my body. I need to express my sexuality and femininity as a celibate.' (41)

An embodied celibacy demands further exploration and encounter with human intimacy and sexual expression.

> 'I must say it's always been a mystery to me how I have been created to be such a loving woman and such a feeling person and then not to have been called to a way of life that is consonant with it, to freely express that in full sexual relationship."' (39)

Such reflection requires that celibates refocus their life project away from only external behaviour and spiritualised detachment to a total concentration of their personhood on union with God. This happens *through* their sexuality not by abandoning it as some 'part of themselves' beyond God's saving action.

> 'Am I suppressing and repressing stuff, failing to take on board my full sexuality? I'm terrified of being celibate for the wrong reason – for fear of sex reasons. It's very important for me to do it for honest reasons. If anything drove me out of celibacy it would be the conviction that it's delusion – that God has no interest in my refraining from sex whatsoever, and I sometimes suspect he/she hasn't.' (56)

While the need for passion and commitment varies with different human persons and relationships, intimacy is essential for human emotional and spiritual growth. Margaret Smith's comparative study of emotional loneliness in married and celibate women indicates 'the degree of intimacy of a person's most important relationship' is crucial.[10] Intimacy and its sexual implications are theological as well as practical agenda for an embodied celibacy. Avoidance of the reality of human personhood by continued denial of sexuality reduces the celibate to being a distortion, not a reflection of the love of the Creator God.

So far this contrast of sexually-embodied celibacy with the negation of sexuality in past theology of celibacy has only redressed the 'dualistic' imbalance. Another effect of dualism is the focus on orgasmic sex, a genital fixation over other expressions of sex. 'What is not so often understood is that genitality is the culminating development of sexuality which completes its elaboration in the adult. It does not replace the earlier forms of sexuality but complements them.'[11] Foregoing this genital fixation celibacy could embody other expressions of the diffuse range of human sexual pleasures:[12] 'growth in sensuousness is also marked by the diffusion of the erotic throughout the entire body. If the narrowing of sexuality's focus to the genitals is a mark of alienated sexuality, its diffusion throughout the body reflects its sanctification'.[13] Such awareness would highlight the fundamental difference between women's experi-

---

10 Margaret Smith, *The Relative Contributions of Personality, Social Network, and Cognitive Processes to the Experience of Loneliness in Mature Aged Women*, unpublished thesis, Melbourne: Swinburne Institute of Technology, 1988, 45.
11 Greer, 212.
12 'It may also be conceivable that celibate people, sexually alive, but not expressing that sexuality genitally in a committed relationship, might so learn the language of touch that they experience more subtle vibrations of pleasure so intensely that orgasm would become an unnoticed irrelevance.' J. Cotter, Homosexual and Holy, *The Way* 28, 1988, 240.
13 Nelson, 91.

ence of sexuality and the male sexual dynamic of tension and release. Women's sexuality is more diffuse and continuous[14] and 'seems more intimately connected to relationship than men's'.[15]

By continually seeing celibacy in contrast to marriage, celibates themselves have become overly focused on genital renunciation. Celibates have a different experience of human sexuality rather than no sexual experience. Awareness that celibate existence is sexual could challenge Christian dualism about sex and begin to address the problem that 'our so-called "Christian sexual ethics" is really an ethics of marriage rather than a sexual ethics?'[16] The love relationship of the *Song of Songs* is a call from revelation to be open to the fullest meaning of human sexuality intended by the God of life.

Political celibacy

A private and individualistic celibacy does not comply with the public nature of the vow. Celibacy requires a public consciousness otherwise it risks being merely a selfish expression of discipleship. Thomas Aquinas insisted that celibacy was only permissible for reasons beyond self-interest.[17] Yet a privatistic theological understanding of celibacy prevails in many Vatican documents on the religious life. While the doctrine of the Incarnation emphasises that Jesus became human and lived in a

14 Greer, 213.
15 Schaef, 48.
16 K. Kelly, Tested and Found Wanting, *The Tablet*, 1 October 1988, 1120.
17 Thomas Aquinas, *Summa Theologiae* IIa IIae q 152 a 2, 3, 4.

political reality, too often following Christ has not involved such public consciousness. The removal of Christianity to a private religion, in reaction to the excesses of post-Constantinian Church-State identification, is entrenched and is expressed in many ways. Such withdrawal persists despite Vatican II's demand from *The Church in the Modern World* that faith is lived in the midst of modern society not in escape from it.

While the religious life has always had a public dimension through its service to church and people, celibacy is usually described as personal. For Johannes Metz 'all we have is an abridged form if the business of following Christ is consciously restricted to individual moral behaviour'.[18] There is a close connection between attitude to the body and attitude to the world. Self-acceptance and self-transcendence rely on a positive awareness of one's body and the ability to risk this in the company of others. James Nelson believes that 'the resurrection of the body in self-acceptance seems to bring with it a new openness to the world itself'.[19]

Much of this recourse to a personal celibacy is an outcome of a dualist fear of the body. Many sisters commented that they could not share their experiences of celibacy for fear of judgment or inciting condescending curiosity. Their bodily experience had become extremely personal, due largely to an inability to explain their celibacy in any adequate terms to others.

> 'People ask you about it, and I really don't know what to say — what are the words you use to talk about these

---

18 J. Metz, *Followers of Christ*, London: Burns and Oates, 1978, 41.
19 Nelson, 84.

sorts of things, it's such an *inside* kind of thing. You know the kind of people who ask you questions about being celibate, you don't even know them. They take it up with you like "cocktail party talk" or something.' (39)

Feminist writers have detected that the categorisation of women as private figures (as opposed to males being public figures) has much to do with male control of women's bodies through motherhood and domesticity.

> Men's ultimate fear is the threat posed by all dimensions, degrees and manifestations of women's personal and political movement toward and for each other.[20]

This has also had its influence on celibate women. Traditional male fear of women's sexuality is not relieved by celibacy. There is a powerful mystique attached to virgins.[21] This extends to all women. The withdrawal of women is a threat that provokes male control. The comparable self-segregation of men into groups without women is seldom questioned or judged, and is celebrated as normal, even necessary.[22]

Through history, celibacy has given a minority of women an alternative to the restriction of marriage. It has also provided these women with opportunities for public careers and womanly expression of personal and corporate skills,

---

20 Janice Raymond, *A Passion for Friends*, London, Women's Press, 1986, 18.
21 'While female virgins held a special place in the community, they were the objects of considerable fear and suspicion by the clergy, who could not look at them in their uncontrolled state without deep misgiving.' Jo Ann McNamara, *A New Song: Celibate Women in the First Three Centuries*, NY: Harrinton Park Press, 1985, 58.
22 This male segregation is seen as the basis of the detachment and misogynism of modern scientific culture, cf David F. Noble, *A World Without Women: The Christian Clerical Culture of Western Science*, NY: Alfred A. Knopf, 1992.

beyond those hidden as marital and domestic.[23] The possibility of such public ministry was the initial attraction of religious life for many of the women interviewed. Yet women celibates have too seldom been able to exercise their power publicly. While their activities have political significance, it is rare to find critical reflection on celibacy's political power to effect social and ecclesial change. Such consciousness is usually limited to ministerial availability and mobility. The relegation of celibacy into private niche existence has seriously restricted women's awareness of the public worth of their celibacy.

Inclusive celibacy

Because women's experience of celibacy is ignored, the dualistic disembodiment and private theology of celibacy has been maintained. The silence of women celibates has tuned out any tones other than the plainchant of otherworldly theology. The universalising of male experience to describe celibate experience, not only excludes women celibates but has kept the lid on the political possibilities of a theology of celibacy. A more inclusive theology of celibacy is needed.

---

[23] 'A paradoxical category of women and workers, removed from biological reproduction, not furnishing sexual services, nuns escape what Delphy has called familial exploitation (1980, 33), which differentiates them from lay women.' Danielle Juteau and Nicole Laurin, From Nuns to Surrogate Mothers: Evolution of the Forms of the Appropriation of Women, *Feminist Issues* 9, 1989, 14. This study further explores how the revolution in women's paid employment has only served to extend 'sexage' (or gender oppression) to force all women to be workers as well as mothers and sex partners and non-reproductive women and workers, e.g. nuns and spinsters, into 'mothers' or carers/nurturers. 'At the end of this reorganization of our appropriation, we are all now nuns. In addition, at the same time we are all wives, lovers, mothers, housekeepers, volunteer workers, and paid workers.' *ibid.*, 35.

An inclusive theology of celibacy would cease to define celibacy against other lifestyles. Then the long-needed dialogue between celibates and others Christians could proceed without the constant apologies and counter-assertions that currently dog discussions on key issues of sexual morality and ministry. Traditional theology of celibacy has been essentially eschatological in its focus, largely because its dominant male understanding sees in eschatology an escape from sex, birth and death 'for which women as Eve and mother are made responsible'.[24] In contrast, the strong incarnational trend, expressed by the sisters interviewed, could be expressed in theological reflection with other Christian lifestyles.

> 'It's probably good for married people to live in a world along with celibates. We really ought to be churched together and talking about that aspect of our life together.' (48)

This would allow a more reciprocating renewal of that early post-Vatican II interrelating with lay persons that freed many celibate women from their former institutional isolation.

> 'I reach out to people, celibacy and my needs don't hold me back. I think I've learnt far more from other men and women – their faith, firstly about themselves – their very honest reactions.' (42)

> 'In the past our dealing with people was cold and harsh, whereas today our dealing with people has become softer and gentler. We experience that we now know what it is to love.' (46)

> 'My friends are people that have the same sense of fidelity – they're not all nuns, not all women, but different sorts

---

24 Ruether, *Sexism and God-Talk*, 144.

of people. Those relationships are absolutely important to me, I couldn't live without them.' (39)

'It's always been other people, not religious or Church people, whom I find myself wanting to be with, to learn from and to share the really important things I believe in.' (62)

Inclusive celibacy also opens up the theology of celibacy to women's consciousness. Celibate women have needed to reclaim their bodies and sexuality at the same time as other women have needed to transcend their bodies in order to claim a personal identity too long exclusively determined by their biology: 'a body objectified for the other had become objectified for the self; and too simple interpretations of bodily structures led to conclusions about women's identity which were in contradiction to women's own experience.'[25] Subjective reclaiming of their bodies and experience is the mutual task of all women. Women need to redress the powerlessness of being defined by others and find new directions 'to integrate embodiment with personal selfhood and womanhood'.[26] Inclusion of celibate women's experience alongside the experience of other women broadens all women's experience and fuller understanding of human personhood. The theological consequences of this have yet to emerge, but it has begun in the experience of many sisters interviewed.

'I understand what a lot of women feel like when a relationship closes off socially as well as personally. You're left outside a network where a single woman isn't as

---

[25] Margaret Farley, New Patterns of Relationship: Beginnings of a Moral Revolution, *Women: New Dimensions*, W.J. Burghardt ed., NY: Paulist, 1977, 60.
[26] Farley, New Patterns of Relationship, 61.

included as a married couple.This gives me a great sense of understanding and compassion and solidarity and ordinariness. Being celibate seems a lot more like being ordinary than being exalted.' (56)

This inclusion would also act as a reality template for celibate women's understanding of their sexual embodiment. There is need for a check on the romanticising of the unknown that usually marks a transition from one ideological pattern to another. For example, too often religious celibate women appear to other women to be free of what burdens them; likewise, married life can appear ideally all-fulfilling to religious celibates.

Just as the erotic sensuousness of the *Song of Songs* was spiritualised into an allegory of disembodied and asexual union with God, making it into a safe metaphor for celibacy, so the same dualist body-denying rejected the sexual essence of human existence and created a distorted celibacy founded on a theology renunciation. Modern understanding of human sexuality rejects centuries of Christian hostility to sex, especially women's sexuality. For celibacy to be a sign of God's love and to direct humanity to its fullness as realised in the promise or kingdom of God it must be more visible. It will not be seen by a world tired of Christianity's negative regard for sex. In contrast, the lovers in the *Song of Songs* experience love as an alternative to the negative experience of sexuality. How can celibacy signal God's love instead of only the negative view of sexuality? Any theology of celibacy sourced from the *Song of Songs* cannot continue to avoid its approval of human sexuality and its belief that this embodied sexual love conquers all negative use of sex. An embodied understanding of celibacy is needed that is open to sexuality at the same time as it rejects the exploitation and escapism that distorts sexual experience.

4

Socio-theology of women's celibacy

> *'There is no mark on the wall
> to measure the precise height
> of women.'*
>
> Virginia Woolf[1]

Looking at celibacy from a women's perspective demands a theological approach that employs women's ways of understanding as well as revealing women's insights. Feminist theology incorporates women's experience as the necessary starting-point of its reflection. Women's experience is both the process and the content of theologising by women. Mary Daly labels this 'spooking' and 'spinning': uncovering the hidden histories (her-stories) of women, and re-generating women's consciousness through critical dialogue with this experience.[2] Women's experience of celibacy requires a theological approach that engages with the full breadth of women's relational experience a 'socio-theology' of the variety of women's roles and ways of belonging.

Humans find it easier merely to replace one way of understanding with another, than to effect real change

---

1 Virginia Woolf, *A Room of One's Own*, London, Penguin, 1993, 77.
2 Mary Daly, *Gyn/Ecology*, London: Women's Press, 1978, 318, 320.

across the complex relations that make up social and sexual human experience. Then the opposite is uncritically idealised as desirable. Thus in reaction to the disembodiment of celibacy we idealise the body and genital sexuality and simplistically avoid the 'negativity' of celibacy. For example, some interviewed sisters recalled the period after the initial Vatican II changes to religious life as being times of having to prove one's capacity to be feminine and attractive to males.

Visible and intimate heterosexual relationships became obligatory as proof of the humanity of the celibate. To avoid the doubt or accusation of being frigid, many sisters felt obliged to have male friends or to invent them. Others found this compulsion conflicted with their understanding of celibacy:

> 'Some would *measure* their celibacy, to be more feminine than the rest of us flirting. You didn't have a natural warm relationship with a man or a priest, you had a crush on him. This celibacy tended to make you particularly cynical about relationships with men. I was very critical between 18-34 about relationships between sisters and priests or religious brothers – thinking: what are they on about?' (49)

Besides this pressure, idealisation of sexual relations represents for many celibates the 'greener grass on the other side'. Confronted with the need for intimacy, regret for missed opportunities for close relationships and other human disappointments, the religious celibate can idealise sex and partnership as the solution to all their problems. Sheila Murphy observed from her study of two hundred US religious sisters that 'often disenchanted with their work and religious life-style, some turn to sexuality to alleviate loneliness and confusion'.[3]

A theological approach that merely replaces the oppression of disembodied celibacy with a theory of necessary complementarity, that incomplete in their humanity, women and men require a complement, does not transform the previous denial of sexuality. Complementarity and separatism are too easy solutions to the complexities of human sexual needs.[4] They each deny that human beings, particularly women, have any way to act or think other than as an opposite or complement, defined exclusively *by* the other.

A holistic view of humanity presumes that sexuality cannot be separated from the rest of a person's humanity. The problem for celibacy, therefore, is not to fixate on sex, in reversal of its earlier denial, but to recognise its incorporation in celibate (as in all human) personhood and relationships. In this women's experience offers a different viewpoint to that exclusive and dominant focus on genital sexuality that is more common for males. 'We do not assume that each and every relationship must be sexual, nor do we view everything we do and everyone we meet as having some sexual significance. In fact, women do not define the world in sexual terms.'[5] A women's theological

---

[3] Sheila Murphy, *Midlife Wanderer: The Woman Religious in Midlife Transition*, Whitinsville, Affirmation Books, 1989, 141.

[4] In the end complementarity becomes a theory of androgyny espoused by Nelson and others. Its inappropriateness from a women's perspective is best presented by Ruether in *Sexism and God Talk*, 111: 'We need to affirm not the confusing concept of androgyny but rather that all humans possess a full equivalent of human nature and personhood as male and female'. The self-orientation of radical separatism makes it fundamentally incompatible with Christianity, despite the historical separatism practised in many female religious orders prior to Vatican II.

[5] Anne Wilson Schaef, *Women's Reality*, San Francisco: Harper and Row, 1981, 47. She also identifies the lack of a 'theology of differences' as an

view of sexuality would incorporate this holistic view of women's relationships and provide a context for understanding the experience of celibacy.

To dismiss celibacy as a no longer valid nor natural lifestyle because it appears to devalue genital sexual expression is, again, merely a reversal, not a serious encounter with the implications of Vatican II's universal call to holiness. Biological determinism assumes many forms. To assert the goodness of human sexuality does not require that abstinence be seen as negative, except in dualistic thinking. Women's celibacy occurs as a natural alternative to the majority lifestyle of motherhood and partnering, not as unnatural rejection of that lifestyle. Similarly, a scan of women's social context enlarges this understanding of celibacy. Other women's experiences inform and locate celibacy beyond the narrow limitations of comparison with marriage, and relieve the dichotomising results of such comparison. Equally, religious celibacy has a contribution to make to an expanded view of women's roles and bonding that are developing throughout society today. This theological reflection depends on the location and interaction of women's experience of celibacy within the wider context of women's studies.

The advantage of applying feminist theology to women's experience of celibacy lies in its methodological continuity: revealing women's insights through reflection on women's ways of knowing.[6] Feminist theological method makes a fundamental commitment to grounding its process in

---

ideological support for the myth 'that *the White Male System is the only thing that exists*'.

6 Cf. Mary Field Belenky et al., *Women's Ways of Knowing: The Development of Self, Voice and Mind*, NY: Basic, 1986.

women's experience. Madonna Kolbenschlag identifies this starting-point as reclaiming incarnation, the critical recognition of 'the holiness of our enspirited bodies and the gift of passion as a force to move us onward'.[7] The reclaiming of symbols through the use of imagination is another common feature of women's theologies.[8] There is a metaphorical dimension to the experience of women that is essential to women's ways of interpreting their reality and liberating it from patriarchal limitations. Janice Raymond calls this a dual vision that operates between the tension of possibilities for women and the present limitations. It involves an ability 'to see with the ordinary faculty of sight, that is, to maintain a necessary realism about the conditions of existence, and to see beyond these conditions, that is, to "overleap reality".'[9]

Metaphor and other imaginative uses of language enable this vision. In their inclination to think metaphorically, women have had a way of preserving their experience to appreciate it in or out of season. As Rosemary Ruether observes, this symbolic feature is the most common expression of women's theologising: 'Feminist Christianity doesn't just write theological analysis. Characteristically, it writes new prayers and liturgies'.[10] This feature of 'reclaiming the struggle' requires feminist theology to locate its search within the reality of women's lives. Feminist theologies are

---

7   Regina Bechtle cites Madonna Kolbenschlag's four characteristics of feminist spirituality as a framework for feminist theological method: Theological Trends: Reclaiming the Truth of Women's Lives: Women and Spirituality, *The Way*, 28, 1988, 50-59.
8   Bechtle, 53-4.
9   Janice Raymond.
10 Ruether, Christian Quest for Redemptive Community, *Cross Currents*, XXXVIII, 1988, 15.

committed to a future perspective, a stance of hope. They attempt to envision the elements of this future by reclaiming the community of life,[11] in order to bring it about.

Women's theology is less concerned with developing a prioritised process for theologising than creating a map of essential landmarks and paths that lead between and across the various places of women's experience and understanding. Thus the function of women's theological method is to mark out signposts 'in this motherless geography'[12], to find a place or context for women's experience of humanity. Women's experience of celibacy requires a place in which to understand its relationship to the varieties of women's experience and from whence to theologise on its particular contribution to the struggle of all women towards the fullness of humanity. A socio-theology of women's experience attempts to map the place of celibacy in the wider social context of women's bonding and doing, and from that to explore its meaning.

Women reclaiming the incarnation

The doctrine of the incarnation challenges us to begin our reflection on our relationship with God and ourselves from within our ordinary reality, in the faith that God reveals through human experience and within the terms of that experience. Women's experience of celibacy, too, needs to be understood primarily in its own terms without obligatory reference to marriage and other lifestyles. Women's celibacy can be seen as a naturally occurring phenomenon, valuable

---

11 Bechtle, 57.
12 Elaine Orr, In This Motherless Geography.

in itself quite apart from any contrast with other lifestyles. It needs to be examined not for what it is not, nor for what it aspires to be, but for what it is in its everyday reality. This means observing how it occurs and how it relates to other lifestyles.

The phenomenon of women's celibacy is seldom accorded the epistemological and experiential value of being a discrete subject in itself. Women religious celibates themselves devalue their experience by reducing it to being always probably as true of or no different from other women's experience. While this self-critical inclination is necessary for any full picture of the unique experience of women's celibacy, it pre-empts valid inquiry and understanding of that reality. Any generalisations about women's experience must account for the obvious variations and differences among women and across groups.[13] Allowing the celibate lifestyle some possibility of distinction would therefore be a necessary pre-condition for a more adequate theologising on celibacy's meaning for women.

The phenomenon of women's celibacy

Given the universal predominance of marriage and sexual partnership, the recurrence of women celibates and non-married women must have some claim to being as natural as human partnering. Historical analysis of the phenomenon of women celibates in Western cultures shows that, religious celibacy provided a protective and validating

---

[13] 'It is difficult to universalize their experience, for women are as uniquely individual as men.' Anne Carr, Theological Anthropology and the Experience of Women, *Chicago Studies* 19, 1980, 114.

structure for an already-existing phenomenon. Jo Ann McNamara's study of the emergence of celibate women in early Christianity shows that 'the virginal ideal was not imposed on women by men fearful of their own sexuality' because 'no early Christian father recommended virginity to women until they had already claimed it as a new role for themselves in Christian society'.[14] That some women in Christian societies wished to avoid the difficulties faced by women in patriarchal marriages or arranged marriages does not wholly account for their choice of anchorite, monastic and beguine lifestyles as their only alternative. There were also the culturally accepted roles of courtesan and prostitute that afforded women of all classes a social position that only prudish historians now ignore. Also high occurrence of maternal death in childbirth and male life-expectancy shortened by war and occupational hazards meant women did not expect long-term marriages. So it is inaccurate to suggest that celibacy offered women the only alternative to long repressive marriages. As Janice Raymond lists there were a number of reasons for upper and lower class women's attraction to convent living: 'Women who were not attracted to marriage, who were drawn by the independence and companionship of women, and who wanted an outlet for talents and work not available to them in the secular world, found in convents a natural habitat'.[15]

---

14 Jo Ann McNamara, *A New Song*, 5; cf. also Peter Brown, *The Body and Society: Men and Women and Sexual Renunciation in Early Christians*, New York: Columbia University Press, 1988, 61, 255 cf. also 59: 'As Christians, women and the uneducated could achieve reputations for sexual abstinence as stunning as those achieved by any cultivated male'. 275-6: 'the world for female piety represented, in reality, a zone of exceptional fluidity and free choice'.
15 Raymond, 83.

That women's celibacy has provided more than just an alternative to undesirable marriage is further supported in the interviews with women celibates. None described herself as actively choosing celibacy against marriage, it was merely one of the conditions of religious life. Given the prevailing biological definition of women prior to the women's movement, the option for spinstership and childlessness had to be a deliberate choice for an alternative expression of womanhood. While a requirement of religious life, and oriented to a lifestyle of service, celibacy is not reducible to a convenience that facilitates access to particular employment and unfettered availability. Thus, many of the sisters interviewed described their current commitment to celibacy as having grown with their own self-understanding.

> 'It's the best way for me to live – knowing that there are other ways, but it's the way *I* choose. It's not tied up with sacrifice for me – it's tied up with being whole and being able to love myself.' (33)

> 'Celibacy made me come to grips with the essential aloneness of myself as a self. I like doing one thing at a time, that's my temperament. Celibacy is part of that in me because it helps with the focusing.' (62)

> 'I wouldn't choose celibacy apart from religious life, but then it's not just taken on because it's part of the life. I see it, more than the vows of poverty and obedience, as really integral to my whole life and loving.' (41)

The most serious challenge to negative explanations of the phenomenon of celibacy is its continuing recurrence. Despite the sexual and vocational freedoms of society today, some women still choose religious celibacy, albeit in reduced numbers to the peak recruitments of the 1950s. Besides the continued occurrence of religious women celibates, there are also increasing numbers of both intentional and involuntary unmarried women.[16]

In a study of over four hundred single women, Penman and Stolk distinguished six groups of unmarried women in younger and later phases of singleness based on their contentment and social responses.[17] These women were tested in terms of their ability to develop a coherent self identity outside of marriage and childbearing. Interestingly, the study concluded that 'marriage and motherhood are not essential to normal personality development nor to psychological well-being' and that 'one close relationship is not only unnecessary but may be less rewarding than a network of intimate relationships' and 'significant activity', i.e., work that is important to the person, remunerated or not.[18]

Penman and Stolk profile one religious sister as an example of an autonomous group, characterised by a consciously chosen single lifestyle and 'a coherent sense of self' but for whom 'work has not been central to the establishment of their sense of identity'. She is presented

---

16 The classification of 'unmarried' is unfortunately negative and dualist, as Robyn Penman and Yvonne Stolk observe: 'She is characterized by the definers of reality in terms of what she lacks. There is no reciprocity in this relationship between the married and unmarried; there are no "*un*single" or "child*ful*" terms in our language'. *Not the Marrying Kind: Single Women in Australia*, Ringwood: Penguin, 1983, 30.
17 The six groups are: the intimate, anxious seekers, adaptive, passive, autonomous and concientious. They range from the younger anxious seekers and intimates, who are distinguished by their need to 'form a permanent affiliation with a male' (anxious seekers) and a wider openness to 'other significant relationships' (intimates); to the later adaptive, passive, autonomous and conscious groups which indicate varied acceptance of singleness and lifestyle responses to it. Penman and Stolk, 122-150.
18 Penman and Stolk, 83, 165-7.

as psychologically mature, capable of intimacy, engaged in relationships and not self-preoccupied. While being single is integral to her religious vocation, 'like all other members of the group, Carol did not choose a single, or religious, way of life because of personal inadequacies'.[19] This identification of a woman celibate with other single women offers a new perspective on the age-old negative definition of the nun and spinster. Most valuable for an explanation of the phenomenon of religious celibacy is Penman and Stolk's conclusion about relationality and identity in autonomous women: 'these women demonstrate the possibility that we raised earlier, that identity can be achieved through emotional distance from people as well as in, and through, relationships'.[20]

This brief survey indicates that celibacy does naturally occur, is less chosen than experienced, and need not impair personal or social development. It also indicates that religious celibacy cannot be explained merely as an outcome of negative moral teaching on women's sexuality. Instead, the whole phenomenon of celibacy in women requires a social description of womanhood that is more complex than the biological understanding of the necessity of motherhood and sexual partnership.

Womanhood: sexuality and procreativity

An important issue for women's celibacy is whether the sexual abstinence it involves prevents the development of full womanhood. A positive view of human sexuality calls

---

19 Penman and Stolk, 141-2, 145.
20 Penman and Stolk, 145.

into question the prohibition on sexual intercourse that is fundamental to religious celibacy. This is a challenge not only to religious celibacy but addressed to all Catholic sexual morality and its emphasis on physicality. By prohibiting non-procreative coitus, the Church inadvertently gives priority to the physical aspects of sexuality and can devalue its relational aspects. This replicates a 'phobic overemphasis' on sex that makes it '*the* most important aspect of a relationship', shading the other equally important aspects of intimacy, self transcendence and love.[21] If womanhood is continually understood in terms of the male and of the other, overemphasis on the physical cannot be avoided. This is because of the tendency to define women's sexuality almost exclusively in terms of its capacity for intercourse and child bearing. As a consequence of such definition, denial of genital sex to a woman amounts to denial of her womanhood. It is this tight equation of womanhood with procreative function that the women's movement of this half century and women's celibacy of many centuries rejects. For women, this rejection is a ground-breaking exodus from the dry-lands of 'the Kingdom of Necessity, from fatalism and infantilism'[22] to the Promised Land of fuller understanding of their humanity.

Many women writers have come to question the mythology of sexual determinism that frames most definitions of womanhood. While male institutions and ideas fail to describe the real lives of women, still they end up determining the language and the experiences we employ to describe ourselves.[23] Schaef argues from extensive

---

21 Schaef, 115-6.
22 Daniel Berrigan, *The Steadfastness of the Saints*, NY: Orbis, 1985, 22.
23 Cited in Adrienne Rich, *Of Woman Born*, NY, Norton, 1977, 42.

clinical experience that 'most women do not attribute the same degree of importance to sex that men do': 'Sex is one and only one aspect of the totality of intimacy and lovemaking... Many women have reported that they participate in sex because of the touching and holding involved and do not consider intercourse the ultimate goal.'[24] If the necessity of sex is largely a male preoccupation, the result of their 'sexualizing the universe', and only adopted by women as part of their enslavement to the 'White Male System' (as Schaef terms it), what is the real role of sex for women? Is it so necessary? If women considered womanhood from our own perspective by thinking through our bodies,[25] how would our sexuality figure? Would it focus so much on genitality? Schaef contrasts the concept of self-transcendence in the male system's foci of self and work with the female system's focus on relationships.

---

24 Schaef, 47-48. There has been considerable attention given to women's dissatisfaction with genital orgasm and intercourse in most recent studies of women's sexuality. As Greer notes: 'Whether women like it or not, current sexual mores are conditioning them to become clitorally centred: their sexuality is being conditioned into the likeness and the counterpart of masculine response'. Greer, 213, cf. also William F. Kraft, *Sexual Dimension of the Celibate Life*, Dublin: Gill & Macmillan, 1979: 'Women are usually more inclined to see genital sex in the light of tenderness, affection and care'. Celibate Genitality, 610-611. This is supported by Lynne Segal, Sensual Uncertainty, or Why the Clitoris is not enough, *Sex and love*, Sue Cartledge and Joanna Ryan eds, London: Women's Press, 1983: 'Sexual behaviour is culturally and historically specific... While there is all sorts of evidence that people need physical comfort (though no evidence for any overriding exclusive need for genital contact), there are an infinite number of ways in which we may (hopefully) receive that contact'. 41.

25 Rich, *Of Woman Born*, 284.

> If one has the self and the work as the centre of his (or her) universe, then one is in a constant state of self-absorption. But if one has relationships at the center of her (or his) universe, then one is constantly focusing on others and, hence, is in a state of transcending the self. Sex may be a vehicle for transcendence; it is not *the* vehicle. Focusing on relationships can be a vehicle of transcendence. That is why it is not necessary for Female System persons to sexualize the universe in order to achieve transcendence.[26]

Given that the experience of female celibates includes relationships in their communal living and in their community service, we could speculate that self-transcendence, found by others in sexual intercourse, could also be satisfied in such relationships. Many sisters interviewed perceived themselves as more engaged with others than they could imagine themselves to be in another lifestyle. While this understanding can lead to avoidance of real intimacy through a spiritualising love for all, it should not be dismissed as devoid of truth. It is widely attested that sexual activity does not supply all the needs of intimacy. Women's experience has more diverse sexual pleasure than men's. This has been especially recognised through child nurturing.[27] Women's celibacy may extend the female expression of sexuality to other non-genital relationships. One reason why women celibates do refrain from sexual intercourse could be that it is not really so central to women's sexuality as has been touted. It is within the ambit of women's celibacy to locate and celebrate the other ways in which women's sexuality is expressed.

---

26 Schaef, 116.
27 Rich, *Of Woman Born*, 183.

Despite the recurrence of childless women, womanhood has been almost exclusively defined in terms of motherhood and procreation. The leisure and contraceptive safety for experiencing sex beyond the fear of pregnancy is such a recent experience for most women. But celibate women have lived another reality for centuries.[28] They have known in their own bodies that procreation does not define womanhood, that women can actively share in creation in ways other than their biological functions, that there is more to women than gynaecology, that women are alive and useful beyond their productivity. While a once-mother can say childbirth is only one feature of the entire process of a woman's life,[29] a celibate or childless woman evokes pity or disdain. Hence the whole range of a woman's life outside of motherhood has been too easily denied. What about all the other roles and ways of belonging performed by women? Why does talk of celibacy only ever elicit comparison with motherhood and marriage? What about sistering, grandmothering, grand-daughtering, aunting, niecing, cousining, neighbouring, befriending, companioning? Feminist writers and some of the sisters interviewed received from non-biological mothers the encouragement to see themselves in wider possibilities. Such mentors strengthened the practical survival of other women over many generations.[30]

Another way of explaining women's celibacy is through the concept of being post-industrial. While all people work,

---

[28] Perhaps older, no longer fertile women have too, but even more than celibate women their experience has been silenced because of their apparent sexual uselessness.
[29] Joan Faber, Female Beyond the Signs, *The Way* 26, 1987, 111.
[30] Rich, *Of Woman Born*, 252, and Raymond, 113.

most people today do not produce or create a product. Artists (between projects), service industry and domestic workers, to name but a few, are all engaged in work that may be measurable and have outcomes, but only indirectly creates products. Yet they are not deemed to be vocationally useless to our society, and while many may have an unconscious yearning to be productive in some way, most will never feel this urge sufficiently to change their occupation to more product-oriented industry. A post-industrial view of celibacy relativises much of the argument for the necessity of genitality, that is, to supply for one's own or someone else's productivity. For women this freedom from definition by functional outcome is particularly essential to their achieving a holistic sense of womanhood. For celibate women to be free of productive and functional limitations has not automatically confirmed in them a holistic sense of their womanhood. Yet their freedom holds the promise of further exploration of their particular (non-biological, non other-defined) possibilities for a different understanding of womanhood.

Self-definition as a non-dualistic way of describing celibacy

Given that sexuality is more than engagement in sexual intercourse, there is still need to explain why some women forego the majority's lifestyle of partnering and procreating. The sisters interviewed failed to provide any common cause. While some recognised their desire for an exclusive partnership, others were convinced they could not be satisfied by nor be faithful to any *one* person. Some expressed reluctance to bear and raise children, while others still longed for their own offspring. Applying Penman and

Stolk's categories,[31] a small number of the older and middle-aged sisters would fit the conscientious group, with its priority on the importance of work, involvement in social and service organisations, and emphasis on family or community more than friends. A larger number would be in the autonomous group, like the sister profiled in the study. Of the middle-aged and under-forty sisters, a significant number would belong to the adaptive group, well-socialised for marriage and motherhood but finding themselves satisfied with their celibacy, having resolved their intimacy and identity needs. Some of the sisters in their fifties also would fit this description. The only groups not represented in this sample were the indecisive or passive groups, but examples of such women religious do occur outside of my sample.

Yet there is something about most women who continue as religious celibates which, while not tested in this study, would appear to be a valid observation about their reasons for being celibate. Many of those sisters interviewed expressed a strong and apparently long experienced consciousness of their self-identity. Other studies conclude that singleness is not a result of a specific early decision, but a condition women eventually become aware of having gradually adopted.[32] Until recent years, the vocational choice for Catholic women was limited to motherhood or the complete contrast of celibate service as religious sisters. The decision for religious celibacy thus differs from other options for singleness in that it has required an earlier, more

---

31 Penman and Stolk, chapters 8 and 9.
32 E. Donelson, Becoming a Single Woman, *Women: A Psychological Perspective*, E. Donelson and J. Gullahom eds, NY: Wiley, 1977; M. McGinnis, *Single: A Woman's View*, New Jersey: Fleming H. Revell, 1974.

intentional, choice for the singleness of religious life than the drift of other women into involuntary or assumed singleness. The decisive factor seems to be an early need to self-define, and not be defined only in relation to others, otherwise, the marriage/motherhood option for devout Catholic women would have been socially and religiously more compelling.

These religious women celibates seem to begin with a disposition, some sense of self or awareness that they are not likely to develop themselves, self-actualise, or realise themselves through particular and permanent partnerships like marriage or through sexual experiences with a variety of others. It cannot be claimed, of course, that all religious sisters have this awareness, or that other women who seek partnership do not also self-define. All women have tended to be defined by their roles and to whom they belong, but feminists insist that this has not allowed women to develop their full personhood. Instead, women need to be defined also in terms of themselves.

> Many women feel that they cannot be whole without a man. We look to men to provide us with wholeness and fill our cavern... Women are often terrified of being alone. Being 'connected' to someone else — a man — ensures their survival. They do not understand that even when no one else is around they are still with someone, themselves.[33]

It is interesting support of this argument about celibate women's preference for self-definition, that Schaef came to such conclusions as a result of the comment of 'a nun in one of my workshops'. Instead of Freud's and Erikson's

---

33 Schaef, 36.

concept of women having an inner space that biologically needs to be filled by man, this sister connected her hole, her absence of other-defined or male fulfilment, with her identity as a woman. Rather than being the source of all her female inadequacies, what Schaef calls 'her Original Sin of Being Born Female', the nun saw her 'hole is my wholeness'. Without her experience of abstinence, she could not be whole.[34]

Self-definition and other-definition are not in opposition as such, except that exclusive other-definition has not been freeing for women. In her poem *Couples*, Kate Jennings captures the urge to self-define in an other-defining social structure:

> couples create obstacle courses to prevent me from doing all sorts of things easily
> couples make sure I'm not comfortable with myself because I'm only half a potential couple
> couples point accusing right index fingers at me
> couples make me guilty of loneliness, insecurity, or worse still, lack of ambition.[35]

An overview of women's sexual and personal development asserts that 'as women mature and grow in love and self-actualization, so their need for intimacy becomes greater than their desire for genitality, for it is that which will most help them maintain their individuality and identity'.[36] I would propose that in women celibates there is a corresponding awareness, not delayed to their mature years, that draws them towards celibacy and away from

---

34 Schaef, 36.
35 Susan Hampton and Kate Llewellyn (eds), *The Penguin Book of Australian Women Poets*, Ringwood: Penguin, 1986, 208.
36 Joan Faber, 111.

genital expression in order to maintain their individuality and identity. This self-definition does not mean a rejection of relationships with others, rather, through its development by interiorisation, it creates an intimacy with the self that deepens accessibility to others. Sheila Murphy concludes similarly:

> Rather than setting her apart from others, the development of an individualized philosophy of life bonds her even more closely to others who have also formulated theirs, for as each religious learns what it means to become most uniquely herself, she also learns that in her human individuality she is most like other persons.[37]

Nevertheless, not all women living religious celibacy develop this initial sense of self, as Murphy continues: 'Like her married sister who delayed developing her personal identity until meeting a man whose identity she could assume, the woman religious forestalled her personal identity search as she learned to accept the identity of her community'.[38]

Women's celibacy is more adequately explained by a wider perspective on the sexual and social contexts of women than as some lack of social development, rejection of sexual expression or denial of full womanhood. This reclaiming the incarnation in the ordinariness of human experience expands our consciousness of women's humanity to include women's experience of celibacy. Celibacy contributes topology and texture to this map of womanhood. One of the sisters interviewed ironically reversed the usual description of celibacy as unnatural with the insight that

---

37 Murphy, 168.
38 Murphy, 120.

celibacy is *the* natural lifestyle: 'the majority of people happen to augment with sexual expression and partnership, on their way to discovering that they eventually need to develop their self-identity'.

Women reclaiming the struggle

More forms of human interaction and bonding are found than are registered for womanhood. This lack of mapping leads women to get lost in the isolation of male-defined relationships and forget their more varied landscape. Mary Daly spoonerises this confusion of directions: 'Where do women "fit in" to this space of stale male-mating, this world of wedded deadlock?'[39] Women's theology reclaims the memory of past struggles and listens from underneath to the 'stories' of the diversity and depth of women's bonding.

While women's celibacy continued as alternative women's bonding, it also lost its sense of direction when blocked by the fear that particular friendships were inevitable detours into dependent or lesbian interaction. As Joan Chittister recalls 'spontaneous relationships between likeminded people were very difficult to develop and easy to identify as violations of detachment. In the name of community, contemplation, and chastity the communal dimensions of celibacy had been abandoned'.[40] A women's theology of celibacy needs to be a place where the search for the variety of women's relationships and roles beyond

---

39 Daly, 52.
40 Joan Chittister, *Climb Along the Cutting Edge: An Analysis of Change in Religious Life*, New York: Paulist, 1977, 191-2. Cf. also the Custom directive of the Sisters of Mercy: 'the Sisters shall not admit any inordinate particular friendships, attachments, or affections among them'.

partner and mother can restart. To explore this sufficiently requires a prior rejection of the fear of latent lesbianism in relationships between women. These relationships and roles deserve to be seen primarily as examples of women's bonding, not as alternatives or threats to heterosexuality. While acknowledging and respecting the lesbian right to designate what fits lesbian experience, this theologising must refuse automatic lesbian labels for all women's interaction, in order to reclaim more the varieties of women's bonding and roles.[41]

The nature of female relationships

Relationships are as central to womanhood as 'a woman's subjectivity is relational'.[42] Despite wide acceptance by feminists of this assertion,[43] it is dangerously close to essentialist pigeon-holing women into the nurture/nature stereotype. As Margaret Farley warns, women need to reject 'romantic returns to organic models of society where woman's relation is determined, each in her own place,

---

[41] While Adrienne Rich challenges the male universalism of compulsory/'compulsive' heterosexuality and claims all women's relationships as part of a 'lesbian continuum', Rich, Compulsory Heterosexuality and Lesbian Existence, *Signs: Journal of Women in Culture and Society* 5, 1980, my approach in this section will follow the allowance of lesbian philosopher Janice Raymond. She recognises women-identified women, who are not lesbian, and their 'female friendships' in their own terms as women's bonding, not sublimations of nor preludes to lesbianism. Raymond, 16-18.

[42] Luise Eichenbaum and Susie Orbach, *Between Women*, NY: Penguin, 1987, 60.

[43] For a brief survey: L. Shannon Jung, Feminism and Spaciality: Ethics and the Recovery of a Hidden Dimension, *Journal of Feminist Studies in Religion* 4, 1988, 63-65.

without regard for free agency or for personal identity and worth that transcend roles'.[44]

Historically, women have related very closely within the physical or emotional restrictions of female ghettoes and social enclosures. It is only in more recent western cultures that women have found themselves isolated from female company. Even those most isolated, like the pioneering women in the predominantly male societies of the Americas, Africa and Australia since European colonisation, were sustained by their sense of a common mission with other isolated women.[45] 'Mothers and daughters, sisters and aunts, friends and neighbours relied on one another for practical and emotional support.'[46] This support involved 'elements of compassion, sympathy and identification',[47] all demanding a closeness and regularity of contact for adequate realisation, but also allowing for the distance of developing individual and social personalities. The greatest cause of isolation of women from other women has been the emergence of the nuclear family and urbanisation.

Sisterhood as a women's relationship is scarcely examined in general society and the women's movement, except its use as political equivalent to male brotherhood.[48] While there is extensive reflection on sisters in literature and recent

---

[44] M. Farley, Feminist Consciousness and the Interpretation of Scripture, in Letty Russell (ed.), *Feminist Interpretation of the Bible*, Oxford: Blackwell, 1985, 47.
[45] Jan Carter, *Nothing to Spare: Recollections of Australian Pioneering Women*, Ringwood: Penguin, 1981, 221.
[46] Eichenbaum and Orbach, 31.
[47] Eichenbaum and Orbach, 19.
[48] Of the few studies: Elizabeth Fishel, *Sisters: Loving and Rivalry*, NY: Bantam, 1979; Brigid McConville, *Sisters*, London: Pan, 1985.

cinema, sibling studies concentrate on different gender rivalry rather than on same gender relationships. While the name sister is employed to designate members of women's religious orders, there has been little reflection on the implications of sistering among these members. Religious sisters do relate but not automatically in friendship modes or in sibling roles, yet there is an interaction that at its best goes beyond the level of work-companionship. The interviewed sisters referred more to mothering and nurturing experiences in the context of a maternal hierarchical model of leadership. While consciousness of this sistering role is limited, there is considerable evidence of meaningful bonding among sisters that accompanies the lifestyle and relieves some of its isolation.[49] This bonding is different to friendship in that it represents a wide age and occupational range and may not share many common interests, yet it transcends these and other physical distances in a tribal way of connecting identity. Religious women celibates have developed life-giving support through this relating with each other despite many restrictions on their interaction. Some sisters interviewed spoke of their formative experiences of care, encouragement and role-modelling through the company of women in convent life.

> 'I found a lot of the women in our community cultured and very progressive about women's growth and freedom. They opened up life for me. Particularly the older women, they kind of nurtured me.' (62)

> 'These relationships with women have always been important for me, they've stood out more than relationships with men.' (44)

---

49 Murphy, 141-2.

'With these women I developed a couple of very close relationships, through which I saw a lot of what it is to be a woman and love that.' (55)

Others also referred to the effects of limitations imposed on this relating.

'The more outgoing, warm, loving people tended to be classified as people you had to keep your eye on, make sure they didn't get too close to you. I think that was a very negative response to celibacy. People had innuendos placed around them of lesbian tendencies. And most of that was just the way people responded in a tender, warm way to each other. It encouraged withdrawal.' (49)

'Rather than the danger of friendships, it's lots of friends that holds a group together, lots of friends in the group. If you didn't have friends in the group, who would you come home to? That was the question asked, which was a good, positive thing for people to be saying. Because you're going to make friends somewhere. There should be a place where you can come home to, where you feel good, your friends are going to be there.' (64)

This celibate women's company is given a positive assessment by Janice Raymond:

Nuns gave witness to the fact that there are intense passions of love and friendship besides the sexual/genital. Emotional energy has many forms of intensity. Nuns also knew that the intensity of an intimate friendship is a highly fragile possession and must be allied to other forms of emotional, intellectual, social, and spiritual life if it is to survive.[50]

Murphy observes a more recent development of meaningful bonding as women religious learn to relate more

---

50 Raymond, 112.

openly with other sisters: 'they share hopes and sufferings embracing while forgiving, loving while listening, learning while struggling'.[51]

There is an ambiguity about women's relationships, containing as they do the complexities of as yet not fully understood womanhood. Within layers of mother-daughter, sibling, marriage-market conflicts and rivalries are other urges to identify with, share in, and accompany each other in positive experiences of women's bonding. If 'the original deep adult bonding is that of woman for woman', the importance of women's relationships for the development of self identity, and the role of women, like-selves, in this becomes crucial.[52] Women writers see women supporting each others' autonomy and self-development: 'women affect, move, stir, and arouse each other to full power'.[53] Much of this is sensory as much as social and political. Women often experience themselves as invisible and alone in male company, except as objects of sexual gratification. Being with other women is to be seen, to be recognised, to understand and even to be understood. It is also to sense one's self, not in contrast or inferiority, but in likeness, and to healthily transcend that self, not in self-abnegation, but by recognising differences that are other but not alien. In this way women's bonding allows difference, 'the moving presence of each Self calls forth the living presence of other journeying/enspiriting selves.'[54]

---

51 Murphy, 142.
52 Susan Cavin cited in A. Rich, *Blood, Bread and Poetry: Selected Prose*, NY, W.W. Norton, 1986, 49.
53 Raymond, 229: Eichenbaum and Orbach, 12.
54 Sharon D. Welch, *Communities of Resistance and Solidarity: A Feminist Theology of Liberation*, Maryknoll: Orbis, 1985, 59; Daily, 366.

A woman has the 'capacity to feel herself into someone else's experience and the impulse to take account of others' feelings'.[55] But this is also a cause of insecurity and negation for a woman if she has not distinguished her own needs and therefore fails to find herself, 'because the only mechanism she has for doing so is through merging and identifying with others'.[56] This becomes another form of defining herself exclusively through others. It is claimed that recognising this relational tension is the starting point for the emergence of adult female friendships. When women meet each others' needs but recognise this merged attachment between them, they can extricate their own needs then 'grow, help one another develop confidence, receive love and nurturance, understanding and compassion'.[57] Otherwise they usually only *give* themselves to others, not find themselves. Women friends offer each other the unusual opportunity to experience understanding and affection instead of always giving it. In women's friendship, the other can be as close and familiar as the self. But the other is also sufficiently different that the friendship transcends narcissism. Women friends also experience an otherness that leads beyond oneself in a confident love, and is not just projection of one's needs. 'What distinguishes women's friendships is the easy reciprocity that envelops the relationship, allowing so many things to be safely discussed and felt.'[58]

These references to women's friendship indicate that this way of loving, being and belonging has the most life-giving

---

55 Eichenbaum and Orbach, 61.
56 Eichanbaum and Orbach, 62.
57 Eichenbaum and Orbach, 89.
58 Eichenbaum and Orbach, 21.

and still to be explored potential of all women's relationships. Margaret Farley describes friendship as 'the sustained communion' that allows 'a mutually committed love and sharing of life' and is the direction of all faithful love.[59] Sallie McFague sees friendship's basis in freedom as its advantage over other more intimate or familial relationships; 'all other relationships are ringed with duty or utility or desire.'[60] Friendship is the loving that the Johannine Jesus offered to his companions (John 15:12-17). Friendship reveals more the faithful activity of love that is free, a counter to the passionate flare of more intimate engagement.

> A deep friendship with a woman provides a sense of continuity ... friends are used to fading in and out of the forefront of relationships. Friendship implies an unstated and unworried acceptance frequently missing in love affairs and marriage where the threat of the other leaving (or leaving oneself) often lurks.[61]

In celibate women's lives, friendship has not always functioned to the degree described above. Women religious inadvertently acquire celibacy and women's company as part of their life choice to serve God and be for others. Women's celibacy provides the capacity to move through the tendency for merged attachments by means of the detachment of celibate love. But it is in friendship that the accompanying danger of self-centredness through such detachment is checked. The key to celibate women's friendships with each other is support for the common task of their mission, their relationship with God, and building a better world. As one sister observed, there is a recognition

---

59 Farley, *Personal Commitments*, NY: Harper & Row, 1990, 65.
60 McFague, *Models of God*, 162.
61 Eichenbaum and Orbach, 21.

in this of how celibate women are still discovering the rich potential of their female company.

> 'We need each other's friendship, more now, in order to know our commitment to each other, to our community. Otherwise we don't act out our commitment, we only will it.' (48)

Celibacy of its nature intensifies emotional isolation and loneliness. As Margaret Smith's study of comparative loneliness in married and celibate women indicates:

> while women religious seem to evaluate their social network as satisfactory in terms of the number of relationships they have, they tend to feel dissatisfied with their social network, and tend also to feel a need for greater levels of intimacy in those relationships that are most important to them.[62]

While not detaching the woman celibate from her core transcendental union with God, there would appear to be more scope for women's friendships to develop, in order to benefit from the support of like-minded and like-hearted women.

Janice Raymond presents some vision of the possibilities to be realised in women's friendships in her four conditions of women's friendship: thoughtfulness, passion, worldliness, and happiness. In thoughtfulness, she prepares the ground for a liberative type of loving that both reasons, and is considerate and caring. She is convinced that this thoughtfulness, intention and concern, is what is missing from the aggravated elements of many radical feminist and other women's relations. Ideological purity and physical intensity tend to overwhelm the human need for personal

---

[62] Margaret Smith, 44.

attention and remembering. She emphasises the advantage of more conscious awareness of these in women's relationships. 'Passion is not a feeling that can be isolated from other circumstances in a woman's life.' She presents it as a thoughtful love, not watered-down but 'characterised by strong feeling and, often, physical affection. It is also characterised by proper *timing* and *temperature*'. Worldliness is a deliberate rejection of withdrawal into an interpersonal or self preoccupation, instead of exercising responsible love for all beings and the world. Happiness is mutually seeking the integrity of self, being life-glad.[63] The basis in Christian hope for this vision is clear and acknowledged by her.[64]

The variety and locus of women's relationships

It has been a serious denial of the plurality of our social reality that women's roles have been restricted to mothering and partnering. It is a more serious denial of the diversity of creation and the implications of the incarnation that the wider women's reality is not recognised because of this universalising of male-related roles for women. The gospels depict that women related to Jesus in sufficiently different roles to challenge the authority of this single-laned highway. As nurturers, teachers, debaters, followers, challengers, missionaries, source material, ideas people and faithful supporters, women embodied for the male Jesus of the gospels the fullest meaning of the incarnation. All the

---

63 Raymond, 218-239.
64 Raymond, 211-213.

possible women's roles express possibilities of revealing God's love. Why, then, have celibate women been limited to comparison with mothers and spouses, or by concession termed non-biological mothers? Why have women's diverse ways of showing God's love thus been denied? Why have celibate women not claimed the aunting, cousining, niecing, sistering roles as well as spouse of Christ?

Instead of the myopia of seeing the family as the only model of social unity, the long-sighted and inclusive vision of the kingdom of God needs to be explored. As long as the model of family is promoted exclusively by the Church, many feel locked out of the community of salvation. Celibate women are as excluded as single and deserted women. The Jesus of the gospels clearly rejected giving priority to the family over the wider inclusiveness of the kingdom. In contrast family perpetuates both the obligatory female role of mother and its post-feminist social mutation, cause-orphans: 'women not looking for an ideology so much as a family in which to create an identity for themselves'.[65]

Many women celibates find themselves caught within such idealisation of the family, which their celibacy apparently relinquishes, without any alternative except comparing religious community with the family. Instead of creating family with its often patriarchal and matriarchal limitations and focus on domestic life, celibate women's inter-carnating mission is to create public, equal, mutual and loving communities, opening people and places to include others. This was the radical contribution of early Christianity:

---

65 Joanna Murray-Smith, Lessons of Liberation, *The Age*, 24 June 1989, 12.

Early Christians could not imagine this new humanity of spiritual equality except in some new form of existence that would depart from marriage and procreation, and hence from the patriarchal family. It is in this eschatological or antifamilial form that Christian spiritual egalitarianism is picked up in Christian tradition, in a radical form by groups such as gnostics and Montanists, who were repressed as heretics, and in a modified form, in female monasticism.[66]

Women reclaiming symbols

Another way to understand women's celibacy in a non-dualist way is through the imagination of metaphor, 'creating alternatives, breaking out of impasses and dead ends, finding unexpected solutions'.[67] Re-reading the scriptural sources for the traditional metaphors of celibacy reclaims the symbols that have spoken of women's experience. It also reclaims the dynamic of employing the scriptures for women's theology, not closing off the past to the present, but also not enslaving the present to the limitations of past readings. This use of imagination does not stop at re-appropriating the symbolic images of past communities, it also imagines a women's experience of celibacy that can express the fullness of the love of the women who live it

---

66 Ruether, Sexism as Ideology and Social System: Can Christianity be Liberated from Patriarchy?, *With Both Eyes Open: Seeing Beyond Gender*, P.A. Johnson and J. Kalven eds, NY: Pilgrim, 1988, 158. Cf. also Peter Brown, 53, on the Corinthians' eschatological attitude to marriage: 'Only by dissolving the household was it possible to achieve the priceless transparency associated with the new creation. It is the great hope which, in all future centuries, would continue to flicker disquietingly along the edges of the Christian Church'.
67 Bechtle, 54.

now. It imagines ways to communicate the divine and human sources of that love to the church and world. The imaginative task of a women's theology of celibacy is to locate the other conceptions of God, self, humanity and love that emerge from the celibate experience. What does this lifestyle reveal about God and humanity? What are the possibilities for human relationships revealed by this lifestyle? What is celibate love?

Reclaiming the metaphor of indwelling

The re-symbolising of Christian discipleship through the socialised model of mutual indwelling in John's Gospel, opens a new vision for this women's socio-theology of celibacy. The inclusive, organic and relational nature of this image embodies or incarnates union with God, God's action of salvation and the discipleship that flows from this. It reveals an incarnating God who is relational, connecting with human experience and reconnecting God's relationship with humans and humans' relationships with each other. God becomes synonymous with love (1 Jn 3). Loving is God-like, inclusive, organic, and relational.[68] Oneness with God, a fundamental goal of religious celibacy, is manifested in a discipleship that is inclusive, that enlarges community to be accessible to all regardless of gender, function or rank. Abiding in love is the sole requirement

---

68 Sallie McFague develops this understanding in her portrayal of the second personhood of God as 'God as Lover'. 'We speak of God as love but are afraid to call God lover. But a God who relates to all that is, not distantly and bloodlessly but intimately and passionately, is appropriately called lover', and 'the model of God as lover implies that salvation is the reunification of the beloved world with its lover, God.' *Models of God*, 130, 135.

of this discipleship. Love is the existential expression of this inclusive salvation. It is a love that is organic, involving incarnation and inter-carnation. It re-socialises humans, re-connects them, fosters inter-carnation. This love is not asexual, it is intimate, social and passionate.

The promise of this vision of humanity is a fully satisfying union with God and other humans, not limited by biology, hierarchy, fear or any other force that oppresses. The image of John 16:21 shows this promise emerging from the context of pregnant waiting and the pain and struggle of birthing. Celibacy is another form of discipleship awaiting the fullness of God's promise. In this image of the pregnant struggle that leads up to the kingdom, even the celibate woman can find meaning for her sexual abstinence. She does not reject the fullest expression of her sexuality but is symbolic of the incompleteness of all humans waiting to be fulfilled by God's promise.

Humanity is visioned as capable of re-socialising, of including others while realising self. Partnering is not the sole expression of humanity visioned. Inter-carnating extends human relationships beyond pairing. The uterine metaphor for indwelling, used as a symbol of salvation (Jn 16:21), does not pretend that biological determinism, oppressive relationships, and fears that induce passive and conservative behaviour in women are swept away by Christianity. By locating this symbol of salvation within the common cause of women's biological and social captivity, pregnancy, the reality is acknowledged while the promise is announced. In this sense the metaphor acts not as a pie in the sky ideal, but as a dangerous memory of God's action through the ordinary, even through suffering. Who more than women know the paradox of their sexuality, its capacity to give new life, and its limits on their freedom, even to the threat of death? Who more than celibate women know the paradox of their sexuality, its capacity for freedom and development of womanhood despite self-chosen sterility, loneliness and the restriction of sexual expression?

Celibacy and inclusive love

By re-symbolising Christian discipleship as indwelling love, a dynamic reshaping of celibate love is imagined. All human love seeks union, promises mutuality but is lessened by the fear of its being taken away. Celibacy is an experiment in human love.[69] It anticipates a love where relating is not a risk, is always mutual and is as integrated as indwelling. Celibacy, then is like a metaphor, it is incongruous and unconventional, yet it reveals. It appears to promote a deprived humanity, yet it envisions other ways to be human. It appears to devalue love and sex, yet it seeks other ways to be relational and human. It is an understanding that love itself is a union, not just a desire for union. We desire to be closer to God and other humans, because we already love them. As Margaret Farley says within our

---

69 'Experiment' is used here and hereafter in the sense proposed by Unger: 'The passions are experiments to discover the kind and degree of freedom that a person can hope for. These experiments, however, are also gambles whose outcomes in a concrete life no-one can foresee'. Roberto M. Unger, *Passion: An Essay in Personality*, NY: Free Press, 1984, 114. Celibacy is often portrayed as a passionate life response in traditional theology. Women's experience of celibacy has often denied this passion, but it is the term commonly used by the sisters in the interviews to describe their most personal experiences. This led me to this conceptual link between calibacy-passion-experiment. Since celibacy functions not as an alternative to sexual partnership, nor as an existentially detached lifestyle that is unrelated and only ethereal, it may better be understood as an experimental lifestyle, not opposed to marriage and partnership, but an exercise in the freedom possible for humanity.

desire for fuller union, we already experience union with others. Union is not only a goal of love, 'my loving affirmation unites me with you'.[70]

Celibacy lives out this uniting aspect of love without exclusive union. The great risk of love is the other and their response or lack of response to our love. This is the risk of mutuality. Celibacy relinquishes being someone special for a particular someone. It is to love many, while not expecting the exclusive loving response of any one person. But celibacy can be mere avoidance of being committed to anyone. Like many experiments, it can fail. It will be inconclusive, its premise may even be disproved. But like a metaphor, celibacy is 'a strategy of desperation not decoration'.[71] A love that can be more inclusive, that humans can expect more of than the disappointments and limitations of their own loves, cannot only be hypothesised. Somehow it has to be lived, if experimentally.

An experiment does not occur in a vacuum: it is tested within the context of a control.[72] What, then, is the context of human love that celibacy is experimenting within? In the romantic idealisation of love, love is always equally reciprocated. But human reality, more often than not, is that love is seldom responded to in the degree it is given. Drawing from a variety of human experiences,

---

70 Farley, *Personal Commitments*, 31.
71 McFague, *Models of God*, 33.
72 Margaret Miles suggests this in her analysis of 'separateness and relationships'. 'Perhaps it is necessary that some people in our culture explore these painful commitments to separateness as a corrective for the total investment of self, of longings, of enjoyment in a relationship that most of us who are in our forties or older received as a model as we grew up'. The Courage To Be Alone – In and Out of Marriage, *The Feminist Mystic*, M.E. Giles ed., NY: Crossroad, 1987, 92.

we can find examples of unequal love in which to test the claims of celibate love.

> Anne is a mother who has loved and reared her children even through her marriage breakup, due to her husband's infidelity. Her adult children join a religious sect and reject her, refuse her interest or affection. She still loves them. Despite all, she wishes the very best for them, and cannot cease loving them. They never return her love, leaving her alone, suffering.

> David loves his wife very much, but they have become incompatible. She who supported him through ill-health, ceases to love him, rejects him because of this weakness. He experiences her hate and resentment. While deeply hurt, he continues to believe in the possibility of this love, even though it is not reciprocated.

> Maria dearly loved her husband for all of the sixty-five years she knew him. This love was reciprocated, characterised by their courting manners even into their late septuagenarian years. Then he died. Maria continues to love him, but he cannot return her love. She can only remember his love.

> Catherine has a very close friend she loves. She knows that her friend loves her too, as much as is possible. For Catherine, this is not as much as her love, nor enough for her needs. She goes on loving this friend, not because of the equality of her friend's response to her love, but because of her love for her friend.

> After a significant friendship with a friend breaks up harshly, Paul feels hurt, fear, distrust, hatred and then lack of any feeling for her. Later he recalls a beautiful gift he had fashioned and given her. For love of her, into its production he had put much of himself and his skills. Paul now regrets giving so much of himself. He is reminded though that while that love has ended, it cannot be destroyed, it cannot be taken back. The love in that gift is not discounted by the subsequent experience. He can find that capacity in himself to love and

give again, even though he receives no return for that love given in the past.

Susan loved her husband and children but also fell in love with another man with whom she had an affair. She was very satisfied by him in a way her husband had never been able to love her. She could have continued the affair, or left her husband. She did neither because she felt, despite her love for this man and her relationship with him, a greater commitment to her husband and children. While they will never know the choice involved, in this decision she loved them more than they could ever know or possibly reciprocate, but she goes on loving them.

These are some examples of human relationships where love is given but not equally returned. Many times such love is destroyed for lack of adequate response. All this is the social reality, the context of celibate love. Celibate love is no different nor greater in intensity and breadth of interaction than other loves. There is a great nobility in all love, but the nobility in celibacy is that it is love that intentionally expects no particular response. The celibate intends the type of loving and unloving that most people experience inadvertently. The celibate starts out trying to love this way and, significantly, continues in this love. While she may be sustained by other experiences of love (experiences of God's presence, less exclusive experiences of being loved), a celibate's life, like many other humans, is not about loving that is reciprocated.

Yet celibate love is still union with others, because even desire for such love unites us. In this desire, the celibate *learns* to love through the ways that God loves. It is not that the celibate loves as God loves, but she *learns to love as God loves*. Farley reminds us that the model is 'the *way in which God loves us*, not the way in which we are called to love God'.

> God's love is universal, for all persons; ... respects the concrete reality of persons in their freedom, their life in the world, ... aims at mutuality ... offers an unconditional love that will not withdraw even when friends become enemies.[73]

Celibate love is trying *to learn to love* more as God loves and not to be lessened humanly by the lack of response to that love. Celibacy is a human experiment about how far can humans go without love, without having particular love returned to us? How much can we love without being exclusively loved in response? Celibacy experiments with what is the unchosen condition of many humans who love and go on loving. The intention is to stretch our humanity, to extend its capacity to love without return, while not ignoring the human need for love. It is an experiment only possible within the hope of God's love. The reality of the cost to humans of love unrequited is too horrifying, too painful to pretend at. In this celibacy is a risk-taking confidence that God is love abiding in us. It shows God as dynamic, as love, and all our desire for love and to love. It imagines that God, union with God, union with all whom we love, are not just ideals or future dreams, but already present in our loving, in every human experience of love.

Of particular importance to women is love that unites forever. Their fear of loss most inhibits women's personal and social development. 'Commitment is our way of trying to give a future to a present love.'[74] The meeting point

---

73 Farley, *Personal Commitments*, 130.
74 Farley, *Personal Commitments*, 40.

between persons is a sacred ground that requires some protection from the uncertainties of our futures. The metaphor of uterine indwelling recalls the organic, integral and relational commitment between a mother and her foetal offspring. The image of the uterus recalls a place of protection. The inseparable bonding of indwelling is a vision of how God's love can be with us into our future.

This understanding of committed love suggests another reason why sexual expression in women's celibacy precludes genital intercourse. For a celibate woman, genital involvement would involve an exclusive return of her love. Since 'most women feel that it is difficult to focus their attention and sexual energy with more than one person at a time',[75] this would most likely involve a particular relationship with one other, rather than casual sex without a future. A genital relationship requires a particular other to initiate and develop it. It necessarily excludes others, except as part of a mutual partnership that reaches out to others. In contrast, the celibate seeks to love without any exclusion of others therefore without the mutuality of partnership.

Genital sex is therefore impossible for the woman celibate. It would entail a compromise of celibacy's experiment for humanity, because it would admit that the loveless fate of many humans is too hard to bear. Theologically, humanity would be doomed to hopelessness about human love and its ongoing ability to unite, re-socialise and connect us. God's experiment in becoming love for us would also appear to fail, as human love would be a deceit unable to reflect this incarnational act of salvation. But the social reality is that many humans *do* continue to love despite

---

[75] Schaef, 48.

being unloved. Is this the sign of our salvation, the sign of the kingdom to come, God's promise fulfilled? Celibacy points out that many people do love this way already: the kingdom is here. The hope-risk of celibacy resists the despair that overlooks the nobility of all ordinary loving. Celibacy recognises that while people live and love in silent and loud suffering, they demonstrate there is hope of a love that never dies. Celibacy, then, is a living reminder or amplifier of the hope of love, a joy that can never be taken away (Jn 16:22). God's experiment in loving humanity has a future, pointed out in many lives of love.

Women reclaiming the community of life

Mutual indwelling promises a love that unites us in the present and through commitment into the future. It is this hope of the future, seen from the other end, that celibacy represents. This is celibacy's eschatological perspective. Celibacy attests to the capacity in all humans to stretch beyond our own needs to include others. This would be merely a negative denial of ourselves were there not some vision in this hope. In this hope is a sense of a communal future where the full personhood we seek is no longer defined or experienced in particularity, isolation or fear. It is a hint of a future oneness with God and others. A future sharing in the fullness of love that, having become fully human, is full of humans filled with love. As Elaine Orr envisions:

> Prayers will be said
> for my own homecoming.
> And I will bend
> like bamboo in the wind
> but never break, knowing

> that I and God are One,
> that I am not
> Forsaken.
> And our soprano
> voices will twine like sturdy rope,
> and Our Stories will be written
> in the blood of our own births.[76]

While we do not know the form of this future, we know that the community of life envisioned has to be other than what most humans experience now — not the private agony of loneliness and selfishness, nor the communal tyranny of conformity and anonymity. Part of this vision is being able to see more clearly its signs already present in our lives and hopes. The yearning for belonging and mutuality are such signs.

Beyond households to communities of inclusion

In western society today, part of the identity crisis of humans is their loss of a communal identity. For women, this is particularly acute as they have been so socialised to women's place and its role in sustaining the known world that they find themselves wandering without the direction of shared experience, with nothing other than their own unmapped nascent selfhood. Despite their isolation, our female ancestors did not share our emotional and spiritual lack of direction: their 'private pain was only tolerable because of the overriding sense of purpose presumed by

---

76 Elaine Orr, In This Motherless Geography.

the entire community'.[77]

Modern human social arrangements, like the family, by definition exclude. They leave out the unattached and those who are rejected. A desire for community beyond partnerships, family, and free associations of common interest is an urgent cry of modern humans. But there is a tension in this desire. Humans also desire their personal space, opportunities to express their individuality, and pair bonding that is exclusive to them. But in community we have an unrealised hope that awaits embodiment. Its lack of clear definition and realisation is its appeal over tangible and familiar social organisations that have failed us. Margaret Farley sees a community of life offering 'communal relations that respect the dignity of the individual; global relations that respect the values and structures of unique communities; particular relations that remain open circles and that form human hearts for wider and deeper loves'.[78] Such a vision of the future should have some impact on our present, but only if our desire for mutuality and community is real. Otherwise it is as illusory as any utopia.

Communities of women celibates are not the most encouraging sign of this vision in operation. They are often only households, places of exclusion, as gender and other requirements limit entry. They do not guarantee in their members a communal personhood, that can risk the openness and courage required to really love inclusively. They tend to sustain what already is and not risk all to reach toward what is not yet. But the object of creating community is not for itself, for the celibate's satisfaction, but to

---

77 Carter, 121.
78 Farley, *Personal Commitments*, 129.

support their mission of community-making that transforms the world. There is a teasing paradox in this. Were celibates to construct the ideal community for themselves they would never leave its comfort for their mission. So it is fortunate that the tension between the ideal and the actual life of celibate communities propels them into creating community in the world, rather than exclusively for themselves. Such an argument from paradox, though, does not completely excuse the need for communities to image more the community of God's promise.

The challenge, then, is how households that have doors, fences, gates, keys, commitments, and elaborate means of being unhappy together and avoiding each other's needs can be transformed by love into movements toward the community of life. Can we overcome 'the countless forms of our inability to blend our lives together'?[79] Confining relationships to the models of partnership, family, and tribe, we conveniently define the limits of our human responsibilities to those with whom we comfortably interact. As conflict develops we tend to limit the range of our commitment and responsibility to people who suit us. In contrast, interaction in community enlarges the capacity to bond and share: 'community can help us to understand better the bonds between us; it can remind us to attend to one another and to care for our love'.[80]

Beyond belonging to mutuality

Translation of this hope beyond rhetoric to reality requires mutuality. Even the concept of a community of life suggests

---

79 Farley, *Personal Commitments*, 62.
80 Farley, *Personal Commitments*, 64.

some static ideal to be attained, rather than a dynamic continuously attempted within ordinary lives of love and struggle. When only belonging is our behavioural goal, we fit into the household-style of relationships and measure ourselves against them, offering no more nor less than is required to belong. This is why the communal experiences of celibates can become so dry and painful. We limit our vision to be saved from disappointment. We restrict our loving to avoid rejection. This emphasis is on fitting rather than stretching the limits of human love. An external code replaces the vision of an inclusive, organic and relational love.

Celibacy should not mean the abdication of mutuality as a function of love. Farley observes that even when one's commitment to another is unknown or unaccepted by the other, mutuality is still experienced. 'Something in the other binds me to her or him, calls to me, makes it easier or more difficult for me to be faithful, places in sharp relief the painfulness of the forms of mutuality that are missing.'[81] It is through this incompleteness that the hope for human fullness in love is envisioned, is set free of any mean limitations to protect oneself from disappointment, threat and possible refusal. This is the dynamic that creates the community of life. It is the expectation that years of loneliness and endurance fuel wonderful minutes of giving and sharing.

Mutuality is the recognition of differences, the celebration of likeness, the communication of hope in the oneness yet to be. In the celibate, mutuality creates the future because it gives up the security of the present, the prior

---

81 Farley, *Personal Commitments*, 61.

satisfaction of self and the stagnation of stability for hope. For the struggle to love celibately, without the expectation of returned love, requires a sense of the ultimate that lifts beyond the present belonging and its inherent possessiveness.[82] This sense of the ultimate is developed and sustained through 'memory'.[83] Remembering links us to the vertical community that goes before us, that formed us and revealed to us the possibilities in our present. Remembering links us to the horizontal community of our own experiences of caring and love received, and of pain and suffering that we long to overcome. The memory of experiences of mutuality is also a dynamic force that encourages the community of life. Beverley Wildung Harrison declares that 'radical love creates dangerous precedents and lofty expectations among human beings' because 'those touched by the power of such love tend to develop a reluctance to accept anything less than mutuality and self-respect, anything less than human dignity, anything less than authentic relatedness'.[84] Mutuality moves women's celibate love in a dynamic way beyond the house-keeping orderliness and limitations of household belonging to the adventurous and radical ultimate of the community of life.

While this attempt to consider women's celibacy within its own terms, not in contrast to other female lifestyles,

---

[82] 'There is about the life of a consecrated person an aspect which might be termed ultimate ... s/he is poised at the edge of things and nothing is able to take him/her in and induce in him/her a forgetfulness.' Beverley Stott, *Spiritual Appropriation of the Past from Resentment to Gratitude*, unpublished MA thesis, Pittsburgh, Duquesne University, 1979, 88.
[83] Stott, 88 and Farley, *Personal Commitments*, 63. She also suggests 'relaxation of heart' as necessary for developing mutuality. Unfortunately she does not expand on this.
[84] Beverley Wildung Harrison, *Making the Connections: Essays in Feminist Social Ethics*, Boston: Beacon, 1985, 19.

has been rigorously pursued, the obstacle of male-definition still detours us into dualistic references to partnering and procreation. Even a women's approach to theologising on celibacy cannot avoid the oppositions of this dualism: the definition against, the slight glance over or across the shoulders for who else is on this track. Even the discussion on the community of life strayed back into interpersonal relationships rather than the urgency of the wider political and social reform of women's oppression. While the exploration of different relationships and roles relieved this dichotomising, there is a sense in which the bigger concerns of women's celibacy, its purpose, its public nature and responsibility get overlooked.

There is an intrinsic limitation to focusing on women's experience specifically without adequate resolution of the conflict between female and male systems of understanding. Women's celibacy is itself caught in this dilemma. While its separatism has enhanced women's self-understanding and opportunities for education and employment, it has never unhitched itself from the language and theological concepts of male-definition. Any assertions therefore about womanhood from women's celibate experience are tentative initial struggles against maleness and patriarchy, not yet confident expeditions into wider definition of women. Hence the continual tendency to relate celibate experience negatively against other female and male experience.

The fullness of the future community cannot be fully envisioned from the isolated position and still negative identification of celibate women. Until there is an easier relating between women celibates and their experience, and subsequent ease with the lives of other women and men, the collaboration essential for creating this vision will be wanting.

There is another sense in which this application of women's methodology does not adequately represent the purpose of women's celibacy: a lack of offence. The Johannine model of mutual indwelling encourages an inclusive, compassionate coming together and re-socialising. But celibacy is not always that friendly. It also has an uncomfortable edge, a dangerous jaggedness that bites. It does not fit easily with existing society. It is recklessly close to negative rejection of real human values. It is more passionate than compassionate. While I have been at pains to remove celibacy from a negative dualistic framework, there is a denial aspect to women's celibacy, a prophetic edge that needs to be explored.

5

Ecology of celibacy

*'All things
crowd me in!
I am so wide!*

*After the unshapen
Have I grasped
in everlasting time.*

*I have caught it
It has cast me
wider than wide*

*Me is too narrow
All else!
You know this well
You have been there too.'*
Hadewijch (13th century Flemish Beguine)[1]

Celibacy can be understood in ecological terms as both destroying life and conserving it. While one of its consequences is population control, it also implies wastage of

---

1   Hadewijch, All Things Continue, in Carol Cosman et al., *The Penguin Book of Women Poets*, Harmondsworth: Penguin, 1979.

potential human life. Its renunciation also involves conservation consciousness of the limitations of this world. Together with the vows of poverty and obedience, celibacy avoids the anti-environmental domination and oppression of sex, ownership and unchecked freedom. Nevertheless traditional theology of celibacy demonstrates little ecological consciousness. Some of the interviewed sisters had some ecological understanding of their celibacy.

> 'I regret that sense of the [loss of the] next generation and what right have I to stop that when I think of the whole evolution of life and God present in the world. I see God very much as part of all this ongoing life.' (48)

> 'If I am to be a fulfilled religious celibate woman in this twentieth century, I need to be aware of and committed to the service of Jesus through the needs of humankind, the life of the world and the universe.' (41)

Women naturally experience reality as interconnected. This interconnection gives women's cosmology ecological shape. Traditional celibate cosmology has been more eschatological than ecological. Ecology involves more than the conservation of resources and environmental awareness. It is the relationship of an organism to its environment and its interaction with the other things that make up that environment, its ecosystem. Our development as human beings begins with our recognition of the interconnectedness of humanity and all creation, of humans with other humans, of human efforts and cosmic consequences. 'To realize this is to begin to let go of the familiar individual self or ego, and to experience a sense of identification with wider circles of life.'[2]

---

2   Freya Matthews, Deep Ecology: Where all things are connected, *Habitat*, October 1988, 10.

'Ecology is the study not only of what keeps species extant but what makes them extinct.'[3] Environmental exploitation, waste and destruction eliminate the resources necessary for all life on this planet. Today humanity faces widespread species-annihilation. Celibacy reduces human overpopulation, a major cause of this threat.[4] But this is a secondary result rather than a primary intention of celibacy. Is celibacy more intentionally related to ecological responsibility for the world?

Ecology rejects a functional theory of biology, the view that an organism and its capacities exist solely for human use and exploitation. Similarly, women's celibacy contrasts with the biologism that presumes all women exist for is to be procreative or for sexual use. Celibacy also seeks the transformation of human relationships by relinquishing the satisfaction of the progress imperative, a future controlled through progeny and development, and the power of ownership of others that distorts human bonding.[5] Both the women's and environmental movements recognise the connection between exploitation of women's sexuality and wanton destruction of the earth.[6] Appropriating the earth

---

3   Charles Birch and John B. Cobb, *The Liberation of Life*, Cambridge: CUP, 1981, 29.
4   Paul and Anne Ehrlich and J.P. Holdren, *Ecoscience: Population Resources and Environment*, San Francisco: Freeman, 1977.
5   Brendan Lovett, On Earth as in Heaven: Corresponding to God in Philippine Context, *Pacifica* 2, 1989, 21.
6   'the age-old separation of mind and body may have abetted the inflicting of real damage on the earth'. Naomi R. Goldenburg, Archetypal Theory and the Separation of Mind and Body: Reason enough to turn to Freud, *Journal of Feminist Studies in Religion* 1, 1985, 61; 'A central task of feminist spirituality is experiencing, expressing and bringing about the connectedness of creation, a connectedness seriously endangered by patriarchal polarization and phallocentrism'. Marian Ronan, The Liturgy of Women's Lives: A Call to Celebration, *Cross Currents* XXXVII, 1988, 20.

and its resources as mine to use objectifies nature into a personal possession available for exploitation. The like objectification of sex into a commodity is rejected by celibacy. Traditional theology of celibacy had a negative attitude to human sexuality and to the world. This negative attitude to life and nature is an example of the escapism and exploitation that also motivates destructive human behaviour in the environment. Ecologically, celibacy is not in opposition to other lives but performs a different function in the web of life.

Ecological awareness in Christianity has a surprisingly long, if spasmodic, history. The creation view of God and humanity, most recently recovered by Matthew Fox and Thomas Berry, evidences an alternative spirituality to the prevalent Western Christian theologies of order and domination. Benedictine, Franciscan, Rhineland and other mystics emphasised the human creature's co-existence with all creation. Albert Schweitzer and Teilhard de Chardin represent theological antecedents to the current Creation theologies of Berry and Charles Birch and John Cobb.

Death: the ecological problem

Extensive scientific studies show that the destructive impact of human development on other species, the ecosystem and the climate of earth has reached calamitous proportions in this last part of the twentieth century. The effects of nuclear and fossil-fuelled power, dramatic increases in human populations, mass-production of food, technological monopoly by western consumer lifestyles, swollen waste production and dumping, and widespread defoliation and land misuse are threatening all life on the planet, not just the future of some species. The industrial appropriation of scientific knowledge enabled a world-view of limitless development to promote the utilitarian arrogance of the economic interests of the first world. Humanity's scientific awareness of the interconnectedness of all life on the planet is only now dawning. Only when death is collectively imminent and not just an individual inevitability does this fear of earth extinction become the concern of all.

The ecological problem for humanity then is death, but death as it has never faced before. Humanity has always developed elaborate social rituals and psychological and social denials to avoid the threat of death.[7] More recently, humans have medically postponed death and de-terrorised mass and individual deaths through news media saturation. In contrast, the impending ecological catastrophe forces humanity to confront death. Death intrudes on our antiseptic space through the infestation of the environment.

Humanity has historically defined itself as triumphing over nature. Modern western civilisation epitomises this triumph in its nature-defying industrial and medical technologies. But the irony of such death-avoidance is that humanity is now surrounded with the reality of death to a greater degree than ever before in its history. Human attempts to bring about the death of death have rebounded on us. The mortality humanity sought to avoid through its manipulation of the environment and human physiology has become more invincible, precisely by means of the technologies intended to control and prevent death.

---

[7] Ernest Becker, *The Denial of Death*, NY: Free Press, 1973.

Humanity's capacity for death-dealing not only threatens itself, the planet and the cosmos; it also signals a death of God. It disclaims any cosmic purpose in life beyond what is already nearly destroyed. Instead of co-creating, humanity's efforts to be free have bound it to impending extinction. A God that is rendered helpless in the face of such destruction ceases to be omnipotent and instead becomes a victim of its creature, humanity. Another Dr Frankenstein is overwhelmed by his invention. When omnipotence is the premier characteristic of divinity, humanity requires evidence of a greater power if it is to defer to any greater purpose than its own.[8] In such an out of control climate there is no authority to dissuade a power-lusting human intelligence from its arrogant journey to self-annihilation. The ecological problem suggests such godlike power is death-like not life-giving. The ecological problem of death becomes for humanity also a theological problem. If humans can destroy creation, what is left of the God of life? If avoiding death actually intensifies death's power, how is humanity free? What does ecological death mean in the light of the Christian message of redemption from sin and death?

Death and sexuality

The ecological problem of death has social effects. Economic and political domination control life by death-dealing

---

[8] Moltmann distinguishes that the modern omnipotent image of God has legitimated the rapacious attitude of humanity to nature more than the anthropocentrism of Judaeo-Christian religion. J. Moltmann, The Ecological Crisis: Peace with Nature, *Colloquium* 20, 1988, 3.

oppression or by physically destroying human lives, local communities and whole countries. When coupled with institutionalised and terrorising violence, power causes death. Systems of structural oppression are actually interrelated, not separate systems. 'Ecological destruction, racism, consumerism, sexism, are all interlocking facets of dominating power that controls us all the more effectively to the extent that we try to localise and particularise it in one structure.'[9] Similarly, one sister observed:

> 'The "sacrilege" of polluting the earth, the raw material of the human creation, so to speak, stands side by side with those social evils like domestic violence, racism, greed, etc. which may indeed owe part of their virulence to this "sacrilege".' (66)

Similarly, the women's movement has identified the destructive influence of sexual domination in the dehumanisation of all society. Dominating power is seldom separable from some death effect, and in the ecological view of life there are widespread and exponential ramifications of this death-dealing. Sexuality and death are traditionally linked. Sexuality and its capacity to reproduce signals both life and death, future and limitation. Women's sexuality is particularly associated with death in patriarchal thinking according to Rosemary Ruether: 'Women as representative of sexual reproduction and motherhood are the bearers of death'.[10] Psychology and religion identify the avoidance of death as a basic drive of human sexuality. The theology

---

9 Lovett, 13.
10 Ruether, *Sexism and God Talk*, 80.

of religious celibacy actively chooses the deathliness of aloneness and non-generativity.

If death is the problem for ecological order, it is incongruous for celibacy voluntarily to promote more death. Celibacy takes on the problem of death by embodying it. To make sense in the horrifying reality of ecological disaster, celibacy's purpose needs to be clarified as more than another negative attitude to life. Otherwise, using a self-chosen, self-destructive deathliness as a way of dealing with the fear of death is as dangerous and ambiguous as is 'fighting fire with fire'.[11] The risk is justified only in the results, and the results of celibacy are far too obscure to measure. An ecological understanding of celibacy requires a clearer identification of its meaning in relation to life as well as death.

> 'Celibacy is essentially understood only in relation to other life issues, eg. love, embodiment and death. Celibacy is about life purpose.' (46)

Extinction celibacy as waste

Before 2000, over twenty per cent of all living species are expected to have become extinct. This only faintly suggests the ecological disorder and losses that are direct consequences of such extinction.[12] 'Extinction is a difficult

---

[11] Gregory of Nyssa's argument in *De Virginate*, 13, is an example of this ambiguity: 'But those who by virginity have desisted from this process have drawn within themselves the boundary line of death, and by their own deed have checked death's advance'.

[12] T. Berry, Technology and the Healing of the Earth, *The Dream of the Earth*, San Francisco, Sierra Club, 1988, 61.

concept to grasp', Thomas Berry explains, because we tend to see it as partial by presuming that all life is renewable. 'It is rather an absolute and final act for which there is no remedy on earth or in heaven.'[13] Because of this difficulty, even in the growing awareness of their environment, humans tend to resist becoming aware of imminent extinction and its immediate implications. This avoidance allows ecological responsibility to be side-stepped as another issue, to be disposed of with partial solutions, political rhetoric, fad products and more pressing economic priorities.

A world so threatened by total extinction is disinterested in or perplexed by the vicarious extinction volunteered by celibates. In this precarious climate, if celibacy clings to its traditional meaning of world renunciation, it cannot be understood as different to any other death-dealing. Celibates also need to distinguish their celibate extinction from the hopelessness of passive resignation and pessimism about the future, otherwise it teeters on escapism. Destructive exploitation of human life and freedom is not recompensed by despairing and disdainful rejection of life by celibates. For celibacy's self-extinction to be understood, another theological justification for such withdrawal from the collective responsibility for continuing life is required.

Celibates find the implications of their choice difficult to own. In the past the celibate's personal extinction has been compensated by new and increasing community membership. New recruits, communal living, shared apostolates and ever-expanding works have cushioned the lack of marriage and progeny. It is only the onset of diminished

---

13 Berry, The Earth Community, *Riverdale Papers: On the Earth Community*, New York: Riverdale Center for Religious Research, 1980, 9.

membership and ageing that has confronted religious life with the radical consequences of celibacy. With no guarantee of generations to follow, and the breakdown of the supportive structures of large membership, the solitariness of the life is heightened. Some of the sisters interviewed understood their voluntary death as life-giving. In contrast, another sister recognised the ecological ambivalence of her life.

> 'Have I done something that really doesn't match the fullness of life? I feel that fullness of life is to do with the sap and the growth and the dying that's in the natural world. So I wonder if in all the meaning of living and dying whether I have done something that isn't pro-life. There again, when I think about the population explosion I wonder if I have done something for life.' (48)

The un-ecological aspect of Christianity

Christianity has ideologically fuelled the control and subjugation of nature through its doctrines of stewardship and redemption just as post-Enlightenment scientific pragmatism has used this theology as a justification for human industry. Human domination of nature in Genesis 1-11 (particularly 1:26-30), the stewardship doctrine, is accused of having propagated theological and historical vandalism on the environment.[14] More recent critical biblical studies disallow this reading as resting on a distorted view of Hebrew anthropology. Humanity's creation in the Genesis accounts is carefully distinguished from the animals, but

---

14 This accusation was first argued by Lynn White, The Historical Roots of the Ecological Crisis, *Science* 155, 1967, 1203-7.

they share the same life source and autonomy.[15] The Priestly tradition in Genesis 1:28-30 is emphatic that humans are only the representatives of God in creation, not capricious landowners but stewards responsible to the Creator.[16] Despite these critical re-evaluations of biblical interpretation, popular consciousness that humans must subjugate nature remains.

Anti-materialist interpretations of the Christian doctrine of redemption also have provided theological licence for destructive development and human disregard for other species.[17] The focus of earlier Hebrew creation theology was replaced with a Manichean association of all material things — especially the human body with its desires and passions — with evil and inferiority. This association concluded that 'salvation is the freeing of the soul from the evil demands of the body, and the ultimate hope is for incorporeal immortality.'[18] All physical things needed to be redeemed by the self-sacrifice of the cross, the physical atonement for sin. Thus much Christian devotion rejected

---

15 J.J. Scullion, Creation and Creature in the Bible, John J. Scullion ed., *God's Creation and Human Responsibility for the Earth*, Melbourne: Polding, 1981, 1-17.
16 Bernard W. Anderson, Creation and Ecology, *Creation in the Old Testament*, B.W. Anderson (ed.), Philadelphia: Fortress, 1984, 163; cf. also Walter Houston, 'And let them have dominion...': Biblical Views of Man in Relation to the Environmental Crisis, *Studia Biblica*, vol 1, 1978, 161-184.
17 This is the argument of Matthew Fox's *Original Blessing*, Sante Fe: Bear & Co., 1983: 'The fall/redemption tradition is profoundly introspective, and introspection does not lead to cosmic relating or cosmic caring or cosmic celebration'. 76. In contrast Wes Granberg-Michaelson sees redemption as the positive extension of creation: 'Redemption promises God's intentions for the creation will be fulfilled'. Earth Keeping: A Theology for Global Sanctification, *Sojourners*, October 1982, 23.
18 Grace Jantzen, *God's World, God's Body*, Philadelphia: Westminster, 1984, 6-7.

the world and developed a spiritualised personal understanding of salvation focused on suffering, instead of being a celebration of nature.

There is another sense in which Christianity has failed ecology. The expectation of resurrection makes death only provisional. The death of life can appear as only temporary. Death is feared and meditated upon, but only as an individual experience, allayed in the believer by the expectation of resurrection from death and eternal life. The destruction and pain of death are too passively accepted when redemption is expected. Belief in the resurrection presumes that all destruction can be reversed. The Christian tendency to attribute the title of death analogously to many experiences other than death also trivialises the impact of real death, particularly the collective death facing us. Such distortions of Christianity's central doctrine represent a failure to locate salvation beyond individualist and anthropocentric preoccupations.

Personal or religious concepts of redemption that avoid confrontation with the realities of death are irresponsible in this climate. This ecological reality marks the end of *deus ex machina* solutions conjured up by an uncommitted bystander God of unlimited power. A deist God whose activity is limited to the beginning of creation is inadequate to the ongoing destructive power unleashed by humanity. 'The transformation of religion involves a rethinking of the nature of God's activity and the meaning of God's power. God's power is the power that makes us and all entities free.'[19]

---

19 Birch, New Wine in New Bottles, *St Mark's Review*, March 1984, 35.

Scientific awareness of life

Ecological consciousness is damning of science's complicity in the economic exploitation of nature. Despite this scientific understanding is needed to contribute strategies for environmental revival. Six major ecological disasters, including Chernobyl and Bhopal, happened in the same weeks the World Commission on Environment and Development met in 1986.[20] These were the outcome of scientific negligence, yet their solution and further prevention also depended on scientific expertise. Theological reflection needs a scientific understanding of the systems of life to get beyond a sentimental and theoretical appreciation to an active and strategic reconciliation with nature.

The scientific awareness of the new physics and biology suggests that the collective and conserving properties of the microscopic organisations of atoms that make up the universe are paradigmatic.[21] Conservation is a quality fundamental to the physical properties of matter and energy.[22] Quantum physics has challenged understanding about nature's basic building blocks, e.g. uniform wave emissions of light. It has established that light transmits both as particles and waves. There is a foundational variation in physical nature that goes beyond functional differentiation.[23] Paul Davies also presents another ecological

---

20 World Commission on Environment and Development, *Our Common Future*, Oxford: OUP, 1987.
21 Birch, New Wine in New Bottles, 34; Andrew Dufner and Robert Russell, Foundations in Physics for Revising the Creation Tradition, *Cry of the Environment*, Philip N. Joranson and Ken Butigan eds., Santa Fe: Bear and Co., 1984, 175.
22 Dufner and Russell, 171.
23 Paul Davies, *God and the New Physics*, London: Penguin, 1984, 59-60.

insight from the origins of the universe. The symmetrical creation of matter and anti-matter from energy suggests that at the big-bang, the theoretical beginning of life, there was a slight excess of material, leftovers of unpaired protons and electrons, that became the formative material for the galaxies, planets and biological life. 'According to this theory, our universe is built out of a tiny residue of unbalanced matter that survives as a relic of the first unthinkably brief moment of existence.'[24]

In biology, such conservation of life from apparent waste is fundamental to the process of ecosystems. An ecosystem is an interdependent biological, chemical and physical environment where abiotic (non-living or inanimate) and biotic (living organisms) components interact. The biotic component is made up of three differently functioning types: producers (eg. plants, algae), consumers (animals), and decomposers (organisms of decay). The decomposers perform the conserving functions of preventing the accumulation of the remains of organisms and transforming these into abiotic elements for re-cycling by other organisms.[25] Even what appears to be waste is part of the conservation and transformation of matter in life systems.

There is a conservationist foundation in nature, revealed in a scientific awareness of life, that both sustains our universe and our life as organisms and also acts as a model for our understanding of life. Teilhard de Chardin recognised this in his concept of complexity-consciousness: 'No element could move and grow except with and by all the

---

24 Davies, 29-30.
25 Paul E. Lutz, Interrelatedness: Ecological Pattern of the Universe, *Cry of the Environment*, 257-9.

others with itself'.[26] The fundamentals of physical creation acknowledge diversity and continuous differentiation while promoting order and interconnectedness. This collectivist and conserving basis to life constructs a more accessible ideological framework for respecting and promoting life than the mechanistic science of the past or the gnostic indifference of theology to material life. This counters the charge that the ecological principles of interrelatedness, intrinsic value, and conversion to relationality are merely sentimental. It challenges a theology of celibacy to re-appraise its anthropocentric agenda and find more scientific images of celibacy in creation.

Celibacy and awareness of life

The principle of conservation operates beyond biology. While celibacy is more often described as waste, a scientific awareness of life also suggests that celibacy can be understood as a conservation of life. This is a tenuous and apparently contradictory assertion as celibacy does not increase or continue another human life. But it may be like the unpaired big bang particles, a life-enabling surplus of life. Has it a function like the decomposers of the ecosystems, neither principally producing nor consuming, but rather converting (what may appear as) waste into energy for other forms of useful life? The paradigm of surplus and conservation in nature reinforces the observation that celibacy is a naturally-occurring lifestyle. It offers analogies for celibate life that are more reflective of modern ecological concerns

---

26 P. Teilhard de Chardin, *The Phenomenon of Man*, London: Collins, 1965, 269.

than the traditional spousal metaphors. Teilhard began such explorations in regard to the nature of human love.

> We are often inclined to think that we have exhausted the various natural forms of love with a man's love for his wife, his children, his friends and to a certain extent for his country. Yet precisely the most fundamental form of passion is missing from this list, the one which, under the pressure of an involuting universe, precipitates the elements one upon the other in the Whole — cosmic affinity and hence cosmic sense. A universal love is not only psychologically possible; it is the only complete and final way in which we are able to love.[27]

There is a need for human lives informed by a theology that promotes human responsibility for all life out of the awareness of human interconnection with the cosmos. Humanity needs not merely to restore an ecological order in its relations with its environment (where that is still possible!) but also to be transformed by its interconnection with all nature. This means conversion from an instrumental and utilitarian concern about what physically supports us to a total involvement with the world of life. Berry regards this as the ultimate task of humanity:

> We have a question of life and death before us; the question, however, not merely of physical survival but of survival in a human mode of being, of survival and development into the true splendor of intelligent, affectionate, imaginative persons living in ecstatic enjoyment of the universe about us... A break, a single destructive antagonism anywhere in the fabric of being is a tear in the heart of every being.[28]

---

27 Teilhard, 293.
28 Berry, The Ecological Age, 1-2.

Awareness of the interconnectedness of life resists abdication to the inevitability of human death-dealing in nature. Celibacy needs to go beyond the metaphysical unscientific romantic view of its commitment to life, to an awareness that interconnects celibacy with life, not separating it from life through its renunciation.

> But Life has strategies still untried and therein lies hope. To trust Life is to be sensitive to the possibilities it offers. It is to be receptive to Life's values ever pressing in on us from all sides and only blocked by us. It is to be open to the compassionate and tender response and to follow one's intuitions. Trust in Life releases human energy that makes it possible to transcend life as it is in order to make life as it could be.[29]

Finding a theological meaning to life through more sexual embodiment and connection with nature, celibacy would recover the long-denied interdependence of spirit and matter in creation. It would recognise 'that spiritual insight surfaces through attention to the body; and that achievement of authentic selfhood and power depends on understanding one's grounding in nature and natural energies'.[30] Life-relating for celibacy involves the bonding and celebrating of what was once deadened by negative separation, and relating to and embracing it to make life. Making life involves more than procreating. Celibate interiorisation of oneness with nature is also creative. Celibates need to check a tendency to see creation and sexuality in too instrumental and utilitarian terms. Celibacy's project is to deepen in celibates their sense of inter-

---

29 Birch and Cobb, *The Liberation of Life*, 330.
30 Carol P. Christ, *Diving Deep and Surfacing*, Boston: Beacon, 1986, 53.

connectedness with all life. As the celibate poet Anne Waugh empathises with the earth:

> The earth knows
> Dark and silent and deeply stirring
> The earth knows
> Feels tugged and tremors of small lightness
>
> Seeds shuffling off old cracked coats
> Tentative and trembling
> searching and seeking out the surfaces
> The earth knows.[31]

By bodily acknowledging an alternative human commitment and contribution to life and the environment, women's celibacy finds an appreciation of the self and the other (person or life-form) as having intrinsic value in themselves. Charles Birch and John Cobb have observed that 'there are some experiences in life that are so precious in themselves as to prove that not everything is a means to some end other than itself'.[32] Life conserves as well as bonds, diversifies as well as produces. The alternative lifestyle of celibacy represents expanding life-giving through promoting diversity. To appreciate their difference as meaningful and not merely instrumental or ethereal is an ecological challenge for women celibates.

> Diversity exists on this planet so different things get done. Because different things need to be done, and there is no distinction between little and big things that need doing, diversity itself has ecological value: it helps life.[33]

---

31 Anne Waugh RSM, *Listen: Journal of the Institute of the Sisters of Mercy of Australia* 8, 1989, 23.
32 Birch and Cobb, 106.
33 Elizabeth Dodson Gray, Eden's Garden Revisited: A Christian Ecological Perspective, *With Both Eyes Open: Seeing Beyond Gender*, P.A. Johnson and J. Kalven eds., NY: Pilgrim, 1988, 41.

For the celibate experience to become immersed in a more ecological understanding of itself, it must self-transform into a more conscious positive valuation of all life. This task is not exclusive to celibates. Nevertheless to be distinguishable from other life-denying activity, celibates need to adopt a cosmic understanding of life that promotes more than just expectation of eschatological satisfaction. This is the givenness of celibacy, to be more integrated with other lifestyles and all life forms through recognising their interconnectedness, rather than their uniqueness.[34] Such celibacy would signal the greater diversity and forms of interconnection of life. Then the celibate understanding of how it is to be alive would demonstrate Mechtilde of Magdeburg's challenge: 'How should one live? Live welcoming to all'.[35]

Celibacy has a prophetic purpose

Jeremiah's celibacy is a powerful source for an ecological theology of celibacy. Jeremiah's adoption of celibacy was a prophetic action in response to the de-generation of religious, social and environmental life in Judah. This is not a twentieth century ecological appropriation, environmental awareness is characteristic of the biblical commit-

---

34 'It is impossible to give oneself to an anonymous number. But if the universe ahead of us assumes a face and a heart, and so to speak personifies itself, then in the atmosphere created by this focus the elemental attraction will immediately blossom. Then, no doubt, under the heightened pressure of an infolding world, the formidable energies of attraction, still dormant between human molecules, will burst forth.' Teilhard de Chardin, *The Phenomenon of Man*, 293-4.
35 *Meditations with Mechtilde of Magdeburg*, Sante Fe: Bear & Co., 1985, 126.

ment to life and covenant.[36] Jeremiah's celibacy radically embraced the full consequences of the people's recklessness. It embodied the suffering and rejection experienced by the people, by the land, and by God. It had offensive power as a prophetic action because it appeared contradictory. What God and prophets are expected to promote is life, not its extinction. The prophetic task was transformed from a sideline judgment on an errant people to a total identification with the degenerating fate of its world.

Jeremiah's celibacy was a life-promoting protest in the shape of self-destruction. It relinquished fruitfulness and well-being to point out the deathliness being accommodated as a pretence for life by the disintegrating community. The prophetic judgment indicated that this community's life was at an end. In this non-generative sign of celibacy, Brueggemann's description of the task of the prophet was dramatically embodied:

> to offer symbols that are adequate to the horror, to bring to public expression those very fears and terrors that have been denied so long and suppressed so deeply, and to speak metaphorically but concretely about the real deathliness that hovers over us and gnaws within us.[37]

Prophetic imagination is another prophetic task enacted in Jeremiah's celibacy. Imagination creates a vision of the promise of life by recognising the inadequacy of the present experience that masquerades as life.[38] It adds the

---

36 Brueggemann, The Earth is the Lord's: A Theology of Earth and Land, *Sojourners*, October 1986, 28.
37 Brueggemann, *The Prophetic Imagination*, 49-50.
38 Cf. also *Hopeful Imagination: Prophetic Voices in Exile*, Philadelphia: Fortress, 1986, 1-3, 10-47; *Hope Within History*, Atlanta: John Knox, 1987, 24-26, 72-91.

eschatological dimension to prophecy. Since his world was in mourning (9:17-22), Jeremiah was commanded to take on sexual abstinence, the most public characteristic action of ritual mourning. But in Jeremiah's celibacy God also envisaged another life beyond the hopelessness of the present. It was a sign of the death of the present and impending future, but also of a more real life waiting to happen. The mourning ritual belonged in the preparation time for the time of joy, the eschaton, when marriage and child-birthing would resume.[39] YHWH's promise in Jeremiah 23:3 creates a vision of a future, unseeable in the present calamity but as real as it is. It is described in terms that echo the Genesis 1 account of creation:

> Then I will gather the remnant of my flock
> out of all of the countries I have driven them,
> and I will bring them back to their fold,
> and they shall be *fruitful and multiply*.

This time of joy is ritually characterised by 'eating and drinking, putting on festal attire, anointing oneself with oil and bathing, and sexual union'.[40] It also suggests the sexual and ecological harmony represented in the relationship of the *Song of Songs*. Joy has a ritual meaning across the Semitic world that is universally associated with sexual union. In rabbinic teaching the eschatological era is marked by such ritual joy.[41] The ritual of joy is also echoed in the kingdom preaching and table companionship of Jesus in

---

39 Gary Anderson, 136.
40 Anderson, 133.
41 This meaning of the term 'joy' is found throughout the rabbinic literature as well as in other Semitic languages of the ancient Near East (Hebrew, Jewish, Aramaic, Syriac and Akkadian).

the New Testament.[42] In John 16:21-22, the time of anticipation is full of pain and suffering but the joy that will last is imaged in childbirth and new life coming into the world. During the barren era of mourning, the prophetic celibate imagination is fertile with the promise of new life to come. In contrast, the degenerating life is so desperate to be fertile that this increases its bondage to the mortal limitations of the present. Thus prophetic imagination embodies an eschatological expectation as well as the tragedy of the present reality.

Catholic tradition has understood life in the kingdom of God to be life without marriage with celibacy seen as prefiguring the relationships of the end-times. This comes from Jesus' reply to the Sadducees dispute with him about the resurrection from the dead in Mark 12:18-27; Matthew 22:23-33; Luke 20:27-38. While this interpretation is not supported by scriptural criticism it has greatly influenced the theology of celibacy. Commentators not so committed to celibacy understand the relevant biblical texts in less particular terms as Jesus outlining the total contrast of life in the Kingdom with the present order.[43] Elisabeth

---

[42] Joachim Jeremias identifies the eschatological banquet or festival (cf. Isa 25:6) with the master's joy in Matthew 25:21,23 and Abraham's rejoicing in John 8:56, *Jesus' Promise to the Nations*, London: SCM Press, 1958, 63 and note 4.

[43] Cf. C.S. Mann: 'The error of the sadducees, for Jesus, was in making the resurrection-life a mere extension in another realm of earthly life and earthly relationships. But the resurrection-life is of a wholly different order... In the resurrection-life, marriage and birth are irrelevant to the discussion'. *Mark*, NY: Anchor Bible, Doubleday, 1980, 475; Dan O. Via: 'world concern or compromise with the world is not the ground for the permanence of marriage but is rather an expression of the hardness of heart that undermines marriage. We see again that the permanence of marriage presupposes an ongoing history which is eschatologically revitalised. Indissoluble marriage is in Mark an eschatological possibility, a possibility resting on

Ecology of celibacy • 147

Schüssler-Fiorenza applies a feminist suspicion that eliminates from the text any reference to celibacy. She interprets Jesus' teaching to mean that current patriarchal systems of marriage and ordered relations between men and women are not maintained in the Kingdom.

> It is not that sexual differentiation and sexuality do not exist in the 'world' of God, but that 'patriarchal marriage is no more', because its function in maintaining and continuing patriarchal economic and religious structures is no longer necessary.[44]

This discrepancy stirs my exegetical suspicion. Why did the traditional theology of celibacy need to be so tied to such an ambiguous sign of an eschatological future, when it has more currency as meaningful existence in the ecological present? In the context of ecological reality and the eschatological relevance of Jeremiah's celibacy, it would appear more appropriate were the theology of celibacy to claim, like Jeremiah, to be embodying the infertility of the present times in hopeful anticipation of the fertility of the end-times. Its meaning would then rather signal the inadequacy of any present expressions of joy, no matter how good and truly life-giving, when compared with the utter joy, yet to come, that no-one can take away.

This would also point to the inadequacy of all partial solutions to the disorder of creation. Much ecological thinking gives the impression that all the disorder apparent in our world will be swept away once humanity is notionally converted to oneness with nature. Nature is idealised

---

the anticipatory actualisation of the kingdom of God and the new creation'. *The Ethics of Mark's Gospel in the Middle of Time*, Philadelphia: Fortress, 1985, 104-5.
44 *In Memory of Her*, 144.

as harmonious and only humanity is judged as being violent towards life. Thus the violence and competition for resources that is the basis of food chains and fear between animals is denied. Such a view refuses to admit that the order of justice and peace for all is not yet present anywhere in our world, even in idealised nature. This is the eschatological *and* ecological reality of celibacy: things are not yet as interconnected, harmonious and just as they can be in the fulfilment of God's promise. Ecological consciousness is vital but cannot yet re-create the world of right order that it imagines.[45] This gives celibacy a two-fold significance: it would, firstly, totally embody the current environmental destruction while, secondly, refuse the equation of the imagination and hope of the immediate reality with the joy-filled unity to come. Celibacy would then not use escapist hope to avoid the tragedy of long-exploited reality.

Celibacy is as much a sign for those who live it, as for those who observe it. The value and meaning of celibacy as sign lies precisely in its being *lived with understanding*. Celibacy needs to embody this ecological meaning. It needs to do so primarily so that those who live it can more wholistically proclaim in their own lives that 'each one of

---

[45] A critique of Birch and Cobb's conclusions comments: 'what they have achieved is a formal or structural wholism, a mental construct that may misleadingly equate interdependence with cooperation and harmony. The establishment of an ecological vision does not itself constitute the healing of a broken ecosphere. ... the whole ... does not exist at present. It is still future. It cannot be experienced. It can only be believed in'. Ted Peters, Creation, Consummation, and the Ethical Imagination, *Cry of the Environment*, 408-9. Cf. also Drew Christiansen on neo-Gnostic notions about Earth wisdom: 'humanity needs to look more searchingly at itself as it is embedded in nature, not turn away to look at nature alone'. Notes on MoralTheology 1989: Ecology, Justice, and Development, *Theological Studies*, 51, 1990, 79.

us carries around the ecological crisis in his or her own body'.[46] In the past, women celibates have not understood how this extinction could be prophetic, unlike the heroism that Becker notes in humans who courageously accept extinction.[47] Women's silence about the costs, suffering and isolation of celibacy has muted the significance of their lives to being objects of curiosity. Celibate women have not expressed to each other and others their particular experience of women's ecological struggle with limitation and mortality.

The private and spiritual condition of celibacy has not allowed it public grief. The anonymity of community life has disguised the utter loneliness of its isolation. The individual barrenness has failed to reflect the collective extinction facing the world.

To claim an ecological purpose for celibacy is not a belated jumping on the green bandwagon. Over the centuries the celibate tradition has exhibited profound ecological awareness: particularly Hildegard of Bingen, Francis of Assisi, Meister Eckhart, Mechtilde of Magdeburg, G.M. Hopkins, and Teilhard de Chardin. This at least suggests some connection between choice of self-extinction and the development of a creation consciousness. The celibate woman needs to trust that her choice of extinction is not without purpose. Like Jeremiah, benefit of the support of others and without any comforting intervention by God,

---

46 Moltmann, 9.
47 Becker, 12.

the celibate prophet must risk taking the creation's side with God. A celibate commitment signals a mediation between human exploitation and the apparent helplessness of nature and God.

For the celibate, this prophetic extinction helps her to see that things are not as they could be. She understands the horror of the collective future through her individual fruitlessness. The unused womb testifies to the sadness of lifelessness, but the offence of celibacy pales in comparison to the greater tragedy of the despoiled earth, the ruptured relationships and the torn hopes of this misused and diseased creation. Yet ironically, celibacy rates greater social disapproval. Celibacy continues to offend non-celibates. It disturbs and repulses them. It is often shrugged off as such a waste. But it is never quite tamed nor explained, and it will not go away. Celibacy is a prophetic sign about the interrelatedness of environmental and social life. It is a partisan sign that takes the side of the Creator and creation against the wasteful and exploitative arrogance of humanity. It permits the extinction of one life in order to signal the immediate danger to all life. Celibacy collapses the hierarchical distinctions of dualism. In celibacy, the private choice has public significance, the personal is relinquished for communal hope, and the human attempts union with the cosmos. Like Jeremiah's prophetic action, women's celibacy particularly puts into public view the 'very fears and terrors that have been denied so long and suppressed so deeply'.[48] Women's infertility continues to be the cause of great shame and anxiety. Programs to correct infertility prejudicially

---

48 Brueggemann, *The Prophetic Imagination*, 50.

focus on the inability of the woman to conceive, more than on male impotence. A childless woman is still an anomaly in human society. Women's celibacy can prophetically challenge the shame and uselessness associated with infertility in women.

The celibate finds in her lifestyle a microcosm of the ecological fate of the world, and how such extinction can be lived beyond escapism or resignation. Lack of generativity has a social and cosmic purpose yet to be communicated more clearly by women celibates. Their private option could develop in them an awareness of a cosmic concern active beyond the self. It could expand the celibate responsibility beyond narrow immediate concerns like one's person, place, and the present, to include the communal, cosmic, and the future.

Embodiment and interconnectedness

While the other theological ways of re-interpreting celibacy understood celibacy largely in terms of its sign-value to others, the ecology of celibacy developed here is more oriented to the subject — the celibate herself. This relinquishes the controlling and intrusive claim to the objectivity of sign by integrating the consciousness of the subject with what it signifies. The value or meaning of the sign of celibacy is also in the celibate's conscious interconnection with all living things. The celibate woman finds a new understanding of her celibacy that adds body to a celibacy of the mind through ecological consciousness of the interconnectedness of all life.

Ecological understanding reveals that God is embodied in the world, not only proclaimed through it: 'God is the most natural entity there is, one in whom all others subsist'.[49] The doctrines of creation of the world and the Incarnation insist that God reveals within our reality, the natural world and human experience. The God vs Nature dichotomy of some Christianity is inadequate to this understanding of God. God has direct and unmediated knowledge of the world. Grace Jantzen argues that the doctrine of omniscience leads us to think of the universe as God's body because 'the idea that God feels every sensation of the universe is no more ridiculous than the idea that God knows every possible item of data'.[50] As human understanding is essentially analogical, we are always operating within anthropomorphic and biomorphic constructs. This does not reduce God to a pantheistic immanence because 'just as humans are embodied but yet transcendent, so also the universe can be the body of a transcendent God'.[51]

Contemplative interiorisation works in women's celibacy to break down the division between spirit and matter, body and soul, that has defined celibacy so narrowly in the past. This is the awareness that emerged in the celibate poet Gerard Manley Hopkins' understanding of human relationship with creation. Through his excruciating sensitivity and celibate aloneness, he appreciated the world within of all life-forms and termed it 'inscape'. He reveals the oneness to be found in a celibate's transformation to interrelatedness in the unifying force of 'instress' – 'searching nature I taste

---

49 Birch, New Wine in New Bottles, 35.
50 Grace Jantzen, 79, 83.
51 Jantzen, 127.

self but at one tankard, that of my own being'.[52] Ecological celibacy calls the celibate 'to selve and instress' the meaning of all life in order to relate to the world, as God does to 'God's body'.

Ecology is a way of seeing life as interconnected and co-responsible, respecting and conserving the intrinsic worth of all, and open to transformation through relationship. So the ecology of celibacy means an approach to life that deepens the celibate's communion with all life. Celibacy is ecological creaturehood. While celibacy is not the purpose of a celibate's life, it focuses that life on love so that the celibate's essential oneness with God and creation becomes known and is lived out. In this sense celibacy, like ecology, can be seen as being about living the oneness of all things. It is a way to live in interrelatedness to all, while not in particular relationships, nor in escapist isolation from others. It is one other way to live toward the fullness of the Creator's promise for all creation, besides the genital-sexual sharing in pro-creation.

In religious life celibacy is also interconnected with the other vows of poverty and obedience. It embodies poverty's orientation away from possession and comfort, and risks obedience's trust in more than independence and power. Celibacy as a lifestyle is not chosen for itself. As many sisters asserted it is found as part of the wider religious life commitment to God and others.

> 'Celibacy is more like poverty for me. It shows that poverty is not just monetary. Part of our poverty is living on your own even in community, living with people you wouldn't choose, doing without.' (58)

---

52 Gerard Manley Hopkins, *Poems and Prose*, W.H. Gardner ed., Harmondsworth: Penguin, 1963, xx-xxi, 145-148.

Hence celibacy integrates the interrelated consciousness of the vowed religious life, while it particularly expresses the consciousness of oneness with others. This ecological orientation to oneness is essential to the purpose and meaning of celibacy. Dorothee Soëlle calls such an orientation 'omnirelatedness' — 'what we come from and what we long for'.[53] It connects quietly. It is often so unobtrusive that others find it surprising that celibate women are not so different at all.

> 'I am living and have been living what a lot of women live through, and that gives me a great sense of understanding, compassion, solidarity and *ordinariness*. Being celibate seems a lot more like being ordinary than being different.' (56)

Within this oneness, celibacy is also different. It does bite. Its aloneness is difficult and dangerously threatens to become total detachment from others. Its separateness appears to reject relationships and to demote the value of other persons. Yet the differentiation underscored by celibacy presents the full meaning of oneness in creation. Unity is neither uniformity nor absorption. The intrinsic value of all life is known through its difference. It has value irrespective of what or to whom it may be related. It diversifies lifestyles. By being both different from and at one with other life forms and lifestyles, celibacy shows how difference need not be inevitably adversarial, but can be relational without fusion or dilution into sameness.

An unexpected example of this is the welcoming of aloneness. Human compulsion to avoid aloneness has

---

53 Dorothee Soëlle, *To Work and to Love: A Theology of Creation*, Philadelphia: Fortress, 1985, 134.

prevented us seeing that 'there are other ways to think of human experience than as persons in relationship'.[54] As a result, humans find themselves packing all of their personal needs into already overloaded relationships. The other's space and identity is not respected. Humans need to recognise their uniqueness as a precondition for really connecting with and loving others. Otherwise relationships tend to be reduced to satisfying the projection of one's needs, overlooking the intrinsic value of the other. Aloneness in the celibate woman's experience is about living out her intrinsic value, understanding herself as unconditionally loved by God, not for what she does, nor for where/with whom she belongs. Margaret Miles declares that a woman especially needs to understand herself 'as primarily constituted at the place [where] I am most alone and therefore most connected, rather than to see myself as the sum of my activities and relationships and dependent on these for my self-image'.[55]

One's ease with being alone is the ecological litmus test for the amount of exploitation occurring in one's relationships. The differentiation found in being alone provides the ecological consciousness necessary to keep life truly interactive, not merely absorbing others into sameness with us. Similarly, interrelatedness keeps human life sufficiently connected to prevent terminal escapism from others. Celibacy in its biting difference and inclusive oneness embodies an ethic that asserts the integrity and uniqueness of each human.

---

54 Margaret R. Miles, The Courage To Be Alone — In and Out of Marriage, IN M.E. Giles ed., *The Feminist Mystic*, New York: Crossroad, 1987, 94, 96.
55 Miles, 99.

After the distancing

Celibacy requires a consciousness that is open to conversion, and open to relationality and to the creative communion that signal God's promise. Celibacy attempts a conscious relationship to life and love, not a flight from the world but a life seeking the connections.

> 'Have we removed ourselves too far? in [our] renunciation? I don't know that celibacy does take you out of the world – it shouldn't because it's for the world.' (66)

Celibacy is a conscious attempt to transform sexuality and interpersonal bonding from the tendency to exclusive or exploitative monopoly of relationships into a wider relationality that frees us for communion with others. In her theology of creation, Soëlle marks consciousness as 'one of the few essential commandments of a new sexual ethics'.[56] She remarks that conservative Christianity has failed to understand the evolutionary/historical development of human sexuality as part of 'our being created for freedom'. Instead it has 'misread God's invitation to participate in the reality of creation as a call to a sort of biologism, as if there were no other way to participate in creation besides procreation'.[57] This argument for a broader ethic of sexual relations beyond the functional focus on procreativity reflects the claims and purpose of embodied and ecological celibacy. Celibacy's consciousness can be seen as evolving our species' sexuality beyond genital obsession and intercourse as the sole form of human union, beyond the gender opposition of heterosexuality and homosexuality,

---

56 Soëlle, 136.
57 Soëlle, 132.

beyond the association of intimacy with exclusiveness and ownership. Celibacy embodies the evolution in humanity of an integrating and diffused experience of human sexual expression.

Celibacy as an experiment conserving and stretching human love also stretches its understanding of the nature of sexuality. Sexual expression can be more diffused and integral than focus on genital sex. Sexuality is part of the person's total response to all life. In an embodied celibacy there is another way to such consciousness to full communion intrinsic and extrinsic with life. Embodied celibacy aims to be an encounter of respect and love with one's intrinsic value and place, not just function, in the whole of creation. Humanity does not necessarily depend on celibates for this consciousness to be developed. The ecological project of celibacy is conversion to a relationality transforming the exploiting and escaping tendency of human relations. At the same time, an ecological understanding of celibacy challenges the dangers of celibacy: the denial of relationships, negativity toward sexuality, and renunciation of the world. Celibacy would then embody Thomas Berry's doxology: 'After the distancing, a new intimacy; after the mechanistic, a greater biological sensitivity; after damaging the earth, a healing'.[58]

---

58   Berry, Technology and the Healing of the Earth, *The Dream of the Earth*, 69.

Conclusion

'feminist consciousness recognizes the importance of women's own experiences a way to understanding; it takes seriously the essential embodiment of human persons; it opens to an ecological view of the value of all of nature and the context of the whole universe; it affirms a mode of collaboration as the primary mode for human interaction.'
Margaret Farley RSM[1]

This study of women's celibacy has emerged from taking seriously women's experience as a way to understanding. Women's experience has theological value and offers distinctive insights for a theological reformulation of celibacy. It illustrates the inadequacy of the body-denying theologies that have narrowed previous understanding of celibacy. It finds further contemporary meaning for women's celibacy from interaction with the wider context of women's social relations. It proposes an ecological celibate consciousness of interrelation and responsibility for all life.

---

[1] Margaret Farley, Feminist Consciousness and Scripture, 44.

A women's celibacy that is body-political fundamentally confronts the spiritualising of celibate life. It challenges recourse to body-denying and privatistic descriptions of celibacy. Theological reflection on women's experience begins with how the celibate incorporates her sexual and social reality. Total bodily experience would be recognised as the locus of interaction and contemplation of the theological enterprise of celibacy: the place, the meeting-point, the receiver, the giver, the reflector, the valuer of love. Traditional celibacy's restrained witness merely hinted at the hidden reservoir of the Creator's love. An embodied and inter-personal celibacy would more dynamically indicate the flow of Creator love through all creature love.

Women's experience of celibacy is necessarily bodily, regardless of whether it is incorporated or denied. Through their cyclic rhythms, women are constantly reminded of their bodies. Women's experience includes a consciousness of body that celibacy need not disallow. A theology conscious of womanhood would reflect on the celibate woman's openness to her sexuality. It would set up a dialogue between the woman's sense of her self as sexual and her conscious option to refrain from genital use of herself. Her abstinence would become a discourse with her sexuality, a conversation with her full being. Her self-understanding would become a language for her body, a vocabulary for its pleasures and a grammar for its relationships. She would uncover what her abstinence reveals to her and to others about the Creator God.

She would continue to open herself to that bonding and creativity developed in relationships with others. She would open her feelings to her genital arousals and sexual needs, recognising their place in her, owning them as part of her, and responding to their promotion of her consciousness of wholeness. She would be constantly challenged to make meaning of her choice about her use of her sexuality. She would need to be vigilant about any tendencies to body-denying, and make all of her self accountable to this positive attitude towards sexuality. She could open herself to opportunities for self-knowledge and actualisation through her body, instead of despite it, or around it. Alert to her bodily desire for expression, she would vary her self-expression according to her needs and rhythms, and to the needs of others. Ever conscious of her body, she would respect its cautions and excesses. She could find ways to integrate her embodied self-awareness into all creation's yearning for union with the Creator. An embodied celibacy would reveal, relate, and reflect another theological understanding of human sexuality.

Women's experience of celibacy is always political as well as social. Interpersonal relations always have the political dimension of power, sharing in it, or contesting it. Since sexuality has been *the* source of women's power, the sexual control of celibacy has political consequences. Celibacy encompasses the power of sexuality within the whole person. Women's celibacy would enable exploration of the power of her whole being, not just through her biological or social function. This wholeness for women refuses the functional obligation of sex. It further refuses those aberrations of human partnership and parenting that partition woman's being into segments for others' use and ownership. Embodied beyond exploitation by others and socialised beyond particularity to one other, women's celibacy proclaims the biological and social freedoms possible for all humanity in the fulfilment of God's promise.

Sexually embodied and socially inclusive celibate women have a particular responsibility to share the reality of their freedom with other women. Unlike the traditional image of women, they have had the advantage of being apparently unowned and autonomous. They need to reject the political accommodation and gender tokenism that label them as examples of women's freedom. What is particular to their historical social autonomy should not be mistaken as evidence of an equality allowed to all women. Historically, women have been exclusively defined as victims: owned and exploited. While also often exploited and self-identified as victims, celibate women know their gender power and have long exercised it creatively.

A politics of celibacy demands a more responsible political awareness that responds to the helplessness of others and also the helpfulness experienced by women together. A politics of women's celibacy requires openness to the power and freedom of relationship with others. It would be more consciously interactive and advocate for self and others. The woman celibate would recognise her personal and corporate power and not shrink from its possibilities. She would be conscious of her usefulness, her freedoms and the dangers of power. She would reflect on her experiences of how she is oppressed and how she oppresses herself and others. Such political awareness of her celibacy would enable her to include herself in the struggle of all women and include their experience in her own struggle. Thus she could embody the saving power of God. She could share the freedom of her sexuality as power for others, not only as private space for self and God. She could draw meaning into and from this personal space of her celibacy for herself as one alone. She could open this personal space to include reflection on her communion with others.

This inter-carnated awareness would require of her a disposition towards mutuality instead of being defined in contrast to the other. 'Who is *not* we?' would replace 'who is *we*?' This would expand her celibate commitment to others beyond merely projected identification with them – 'I'm still human, I'm like you' – and beyond serving them because her life is freer in contrast to theirs – 'I'm more available'. Through her difference and by means of her inclusiveness, she transforms separation from others. She refuses to be other or to objectify the other. Celibacy would be her key to the multi-padlocked door of womanhood – one key, but as needed as every other. She would invert Kassia's image 'A nun – a door unopened' by opening herself. She would reverse centuries of dualist separation from other women by being opened by their keys also. She would subvert separatist exclusion of male humanity by engaging with it. Not because maleness is a necessary complement for her, thereby denying her own full humanity, but because mutual inclusion recognises the diversity of the fullest expression of humanity.

This inclusion could announce the Creator's delight in variety, the Saviour's celebration of fullness, and the Spirit's transformation of loneliness. Her celibacy would transform her de-generative carrying around of the ecological crisis in her own body into carrying around the ecological possibility of just, mutual, non-escapist, non-exploitative inter-relation with all life. Her deepened communion with creation would enlarge her capacity to perceive and reveal to others that God is active, beyond creating and incarnate bonding, is active in all of our connecting, sustaining and befriending of life. In the tired, despoiled reality of our world she could reach down into the well of her life-giving and release 'the dearest freshness deep down things'.[2] The life-giving of her sexuality would not be wasted but conserved to allow God's deeper exploration through her life of what was begun in the act of her creation. In her deepening love of the promised more yet-to-come would resist disguising escapism as hope. A woman's celibacy would cease the futility of being an ambiguous sign of an eschatological future, when it has the potency of being a hopeful tangible sign pointing to and beyond the current state of ecological degeneration.

An embodied, inclusive and ecological women's celibacy opens theology of sexuality beyond the walls of opposition, hierarchy and separation. Through such an understanding of her celibacy, a celibate woman could communicate the intimate, interpersonal and integrating dynamics of her humanity thereby promoting the fullness of all humanity as intended by God. Embodied celibate living and sexuality would signal God's promise of fullness by love and life not taken from (exploitation) but given; not held back (escapism) but given.

---

[2] Hopkins, God's Grandeur.

Bibliography

Becker, Ernest, *The Denial of Death*, New York: Free Press, 1973.

Belenky, Mary Field et al., *Women's Ways of Knowing: The Development of Self, Voice and Mind*, New York: Basic, 1986.

Berrigan, Daniel SJ, *The Steadfastness of the Saints*, New York: Orbis, 1985.

Berry, Thomas CP, *The Dream of the Earth*, San Francisco: Sierra Club, 1988.

Berry, Thomas CP, *Riverdale Papers: On the Earth Community*, New York: Riverdale Center for Religious Research, 1980.

Birch, Charles and Cobb, John B., *The Liberation of Life*, Cambridge: CUP, 1981.

Brenner, A., The Israelite Woman: Social Role and Literary Type in Biblical Narrative, Sheffield: JSOT, 1985.

Bright, John, *Jeremiah*, New York: Anchor Bible, Doubleday, 1965.

Brown, Peter, *The Body and Society: Men and Women and Sexual Renunciation in Early Christianity*, New York: Columbia University Press, 1988.

Brown, Raymond E., *The Churches the Apostles Left Behind*, New York: Paulist, 1984.

Brown, Raymond E., *The Community of the Beloved Disciple*, London: Chapman, 1974.

Brown, Raymond E., *The Gospel According to John*, vol 1, London: Anchor Bible, Chapman, 1966.

Brueggemann, Walter, *Hopeful Imagination: Prophetic Voices in Exile*, Philadelphia: Fortress, 1986.

Brueggemann, Walter, *Hope Within History*, Atlanta: John Knox, 1987.

Brueggemann, Walter, *The Prophetic Imagination*, Philadelphia: Fortress, 1978.

Bultmann, Rudolph, *The Gospel of John*, Philadelphia: Westminster, 1971.

Carter, Jan, *Nothing to Spare: Recollections of Australian Pioneering Women*, Ringwood: Penguin, 1981.

Chittister, Joan et al., *Climb Along the Cutting Edge: An Analysis of Change in Religious Life*, New York: Paulist, 1977.

Cosman, Carol et al., *The Penguin Book of Women Poets*, Harmondsworth: Penguin, 1979.

Cussianovich, Alejandro, *Religious Life and the Poor: Liberation Theology*, Dublin: Gill and Macmillan, 1979.

Daly, Mary, *Gyn/Ecology*, London: Women's Press, 1978.

Davies, Paul, *God and the New Physics*, London: Penguin, 1984.

Dodd, C.H., *The Interpretation of the Fourth Gospel*, Cambridge: C.U.P., 1953.

Douglas, Mary, *Natural Symbols*, Harmondsworth: Penguin, 1973.

Dwyer, Eugene FMS, *Decision, Death and Celibacy*, (Tape Recording), Homebush: Daughters of St Paul, 1982.

Eichenbaum, Luise and Orbach, Susie, *Between Women*, New York: Penguin, 1987.

Ehrlich, Paul R., Anne H., and Holdren, J.P., *Ecoscience: Population Resources and Environment*, San Francisco: Freeman, 1977.

Falk, Marcia, *Love Lyrics from the Bible: A Translation and Literary Study of the Song of Songs*, Sheffield: Almond, 1982.

Farley, Margaret RSM, *Personal Commitments: Beginning, Keeping, Changing*, San Franscisco: Harper and Row, 1986.

Flannery, Austin OP (ed.), *Vatican Council II: The Conciliar and Post Conciliar Documents*, Dublin: Dominican Publications, 1975.

Fox, Matthew, *Original Blessing: A Primer in Creation Spirituality*, Santa Fe: Bear & Co., 1983.

Greer, Germaine, *Sex and Destiny*, London: Picador, 1984.

Hampton, Susan and Llewellyn, Kate (eds), T*he Penguin Book of Australian Women Poets*, Ringwood: Penguin, 1986.

Harrison, Beverley W., *Making the Connections: Essays in Feminist Social Ethics*, Boston: Beacon, 1985.

Holladay, W.L., *Jeremiah 1*, Philadelphia: Hermeneia Commentary, Fortress, 1986.

Hopkins, Gerard M. SJ, *Poems and Prose*, (W.H. Gardner ed.), Harmondsworth: Penguin, 1963.

Jantzen, Grace, *God's World, God's Body*, Philadelphia: Westminster, 1984.

Jeremias, Joachim, *Jesus' Promise to the Nations*, London: SCM Press, 1958.

Joranson, Philip N. and Butigan, Ken (eds), *Cry of the Environment*, Santa Fe: Bear and Co., 1984.

Kraft, William F., *Sexual Dimension of the Celibate Life*, Dublin: Gill & Macmillan, 1979.

Kolmer, Elizabeth ASC, *Religious Women in the United States: A Survey of the Influential Literature from 1950 to 1983*, Wilmington: Michael Glazier, 1984.

Landy, F., *Paradoxes of Paradise: Identity and Difference in the Song of Songs*, Sheffield: Almond, 1983.

Liddell, Henry G. and Scott, Robert, *Greek-English Lexicon*, Oxford: O.U.P., 1966.

Lonergan, Anne and Richards, Caroline (eds), *Thomas Berry and the New Cosmology*, Mystic: Twenty-Third Publications, 1987.

McFague, Sallie, *Metaphorical Theology: Models of God in Religious Language*, Philadelphia: Fortress Press, 1982.

McFague, Sallie, *Models of God: Theology for an Ecological Nuclear Age*, London: SCM Press, 1987.

McFague, Sallie, *Speaking in Parables: A Study in Metaphor and Theology*, Philadelphia: Fortress Press, 1975.

McGinnis, M., *Single: A Woman's View*, New Jersey: Fleming H. Revell, 1974.

McKane, William, *Jeremiah*, vol 1, Edinburgh: T. & T. Clark, 1986.

McNamara, Jo Ann, *A New Song: Celibate Women in the First Three Christian Centuries*, New York: Harrington Park, 1985.

Mann, C.S., *Mark*, New York: Anchor Bible, Doubleday, 1980.

Meeks, Wayne, *The First Urban Christians: The Social World of the Apostle Paul*, New Haven: Yale UP, 1983.

Merton, Thomas, *Contemplation in a World of Action*, New York: Doubleday, 1965.

Metz, Johannes B., *Followers of Christ: The Religious Life and the Church*, London: Burns and Oates, 1978.

Miles, Margaret M., *The Image and Practice of Holiness*, London: SCM Press, 1988.

Moloney, Francis J. SDB, *A Life of Promise: Poverty, Chastity, Obedience*, Wilmington: Glazier, 1984.

Moloney, Francis J. SDB, *Woman: First Among the Faithful*, Melbourne: Dove, 1985.

Murphy, Sheila, *Midlife Wanderer: The Woman Religious in Midlife Transition*, Whitinsville: Affirmation Books, 1983.

Nelson, James B., *Embodiment: An Approach to Sexuality and Christian Theology*, Minneapolis: Augsburg, 1978.

Noble, David F., *A World Without Women: The Christian Clerical Culture of Western Science*, NY, Alfred A. Kopf, 1992.

Penman, Robyn and Stolk, Yvonne, *Not the Marrying Kind: Single Women in Australia*, Ringwood: Penguin, 1983.

Pohier, Jacques, *God – In Fragments*, London: SCM Press, 1985.

Pope, Marvin H., *Song of Songs*, New York: Anchor Bible, Doubleday, 1977.

Rahner, Karl SJ, *Servants of the Lord*, London: Burns and Oates, 1968.

Rahner, Karl SJ, *The Eternal Yes*, Denville: Dimension, 1970.

Raymond, Janice, *A Passion for Friends: Towards a Philosophy of Female Friendship*, London: Women's Press, 1986.

Rich, Adrienne, *Blood, Bread and Poetry: Selected Prose 1979-1985*, NY, Norton, 1986.

Rich, Adrienne, *Of Woman Born*, London: Virago, 1977.

Ricoeur, Paul, *Interpretation Theory: Discourse and the Surplus of Meaning*, Fort Worth: Texas Christian University Press, 1976.

Ruether, Rosemary, *Sexism and God-Talk: Towards a Feminist Theology*, Boston: Beacon, 1983.

Ruether, Rosemary, *To Change the World*, London: SCM Press, 1981.

Russell, Letty M., *Feminist Interpretation of the Bible* (ed.), Oxford: Blackwell, 1985.

Russell, Letty M., *The Future of Partnership*, Philadelphia: Westminster Press, 1979.

Russell, Letty M., *Household of Freedom: Authority in Feminist Theology*, Philadelphia: Westminster Press, 1987.

Russell, Letty M., *Human Liberation in a Feminist Perspective: A Theology*, Philadelphia: Westminster Press, 1974.

Schaef, Anne Wilson, *Women's Reality*, San Francisco: Harper & Row, 1981.

Schillebeeckx, Edward OP, *Celibacy*, New York: Sheed & Ward, 1968.

Schnackenberg, Rudolph, *The Gospel According to St John*, vol 3, New York: Crossroad, 1982.

Schneiders, Sandra IHM, *New Wineskins: Re-Imagining Religious Life Today*, New York: Paulist, 1986.

Schüssler-Fiorenza, Elisabeth, *Bread Not Stone: The Challenge of Feminist Biblical Interpretation*, Boston: Beacon, 1985.

Schüssler-Fiorenza, Elisabeth, *In Memory of Her*, London: SCM Press, 1983.

Scullion, John SJ et al., *God's Creation and Human Responsibility for the Earth*, Melbourne: Polding, 1981.

Smith, Margaret RSM, *The Relative Contributions of Personality, Social Network, and Cognitive Processes to the Experience of Loneliness in Mature Aged Women* (unpublished thesis), Melbourne: Swinburne Institute of Technology, 1988.

Soëlle, Dorothee, *To Work and to Love: A Theology of Creation*, Philadelphia: Fortress, 1985.

Sophocles, E.A., *Greek Lexicon Of the Roman and Byzantine Periods from 146 BC to AD 1100*, New York: Ungar, 1957.

Stott, Beverley RSM, *Spiritual Appropriation of the Past: From Resentment to Gratitude* (unpublished MA thesis), Duquesne: Graduate School Duquesne University, 1979.

Teilhard de Chardin, Pierre SJ, *The Phenomenon of Man*, London: Collins, 1965.

Trible, Phyllis, *God and the Rhetoric of Sexuality*, Philadelphia: Fortress, 1978.

Turner, Naomi CSB, *Which Seed Will Grow?*, Melbourne: Collins/Dove, 1988.

Unger, Roberto M., *Passion: An Essay on Personality*, New York: Free Press, 1984.

Van Breemen, Peter SJ, *Called By Name*, Denville: Dimension, 1976.

Van Kaam, Adrian CSSp, *The Vowed Life*, Denville: Dimension, 1968.

Via, Dan O., *The Ethics of Mark's Gospel in the Middle of Time*, Philadelphia: Fortress, 1985.

Von Rad, Gerhard, *The Message of the Prophets*, London: SCM Press, 1968.

Welch, Sharon D., *Communities of Resistance and Solidarity: A Feminist Theology of Liberation*, NY: Orbis, 1985.

Woodward, Evelyn RSJ, *Poets, Prophets & Pragmatists: A New Challenge to Religious Life*, Blackburn: Collins Dove, 1987.

World Commission on Environment and Development, *Our Common Future*, Oxford: OUP, 1987.

Index

Anderson, Gary, 55,56,145
Berry, Thomas, 132-3,140,157
Birch, Charles
  and Cobb, John, 136,137,141,142,148,152
bride of Christ, 30,32,36,44
Brown, Peter, 84,108
Brown, Raymond, 44,46,47-49
Brueggemann, Walter, 46,60,144,150
Carr, Anne, 83
Carter, Jan, 99,118-9
chastity, 12,16,34,38,39,97
Chittister, Joan, 97
clerical celibacy, 12,16
Daly, Mary, 77,97
Dodd, C.H., 44-45
Ecology,
  environment, 35,53-54,57-59,62,125-132,137,142-3,145,147-8,151, 153-7
Eichenbaum, Luise
  and Orbach, Susie, 98,103,104
extinction, 129,132-3
Faber, Joan, 85,95
Farley, Margaret, 63,64,74,98-9,103,111-12,114-15,120-21,161
Genesis *1-3*, 33,35,38-9,134-5,145
Gospel of John, 32,42-51,109-10,117,124,146
Greer, Germaine, 64,68,69,89
Indwelling,
  abiding, 42,44-6,48-51,109-11,116-17

Jantzen, Grace, 135,152
Jeremiah, 32,52-60,143-45,147,150
Jennings, Kate, 95

McFague, Sallie, 61,104,109
McNamara, Jo Ann, 71,84
marriage, 12,16,18,24,28,30,33-4,38,41,42,44,53-5,69,75,84-6,111,146
metaphor, 29-32,36,41-6,48-51,53,59,61,62,81-2,108,111,112
motherhood, 24,56,71,73,80,86-7,91,93-4,106-7,131
Miles, Margaret, 33,112,155
Moloney, Frank, 47
Murphy, Sheila, 79,96,100,101-2
mutuality, 33,35,37,39-41,42,48,104,106,107,109,111-12,115-20,163
mystical/
   spiritual union, 33,34,42,44

Nelson, James, 36,64-6,68,70,79

Orr, Elaine, 29,82,117-18

Penman, Rosemary
   and Stolk, Yvonne, 86-7,92-3

Raymond, Janice, 71,81,84,98,111,105-6
Rich, Adrienne, 89,90,91,98
Ruether, Rosemary, 32,65,73,79,81,108

Schaef, Anne Wilson, 66,69,89,116
Schnackenberg, R., 47
Schneiders, Sandra, 13,29,30,34,42,45,46
Schüssler-Fiorenza,
   Elisabeth, 47,146-7
Sisters of Mercy, 17,19
Smith, Margaret, 67-8,105
Soëlle, Dorothee, 154,156
Song of Songs, 11,14,32,33,34,35,36-41,69,75,145
spiritual union, 33-4,42,44
spousal/
   nuptial imagery, 11,29,33-4,52,107,140
Stott, Beverley, 122

Trible, Phyllis, 11,35,40

Unger, Roberto, 111

Vatican *II*, 13,15,29,30,52,70,80
Von Rad, G., 53,54
virginity, 16,32,38,42

Waugh, Anne, 142